"Deeply learned and rich in pastoral wisdo
us to understand that hope is a chosen beh.
worthiness of God, who keeps promises through the resilience of the human
spirit. I have been moved and encouraged by this fine work and commend
it to pastors, teachers, and folks in the pew—all living in these challenging
times."

Molly Marshall
Interim President
United Theological Seminary of the Twin Cities

"This timely and lively book on hope is what the despairing world needs now.
J. Daniel Day refuses to descend into the valley of despair, but rather pens a
faith in the future present of God. His literary words are portals to the love
of God in Christ. When readers turn these pages, they will be led to the God
of hope and taste God's tomorrow today, while being reminded, or perhaps
discovering for the first time, that hope does not disappoint."

Luke A. Powery
Dean, Duke University Chapel
Associate Professor of Homiletics, Duke Divinity School

"*Lively Hope* is a kaleidoscope view of how we experience hope, capturing
every light, angle, and reflection within its meaning. Daniel Day redefines
and freshens our understanding while encouraging us to see every hue and to
look beyond the words on the page to discover the newness of lively hope."

Daynette Snead Perez
Domestic Disaster Response Manager
Cooperative Baptist Fellowship

"The gift Christians have to offer to the world is the hope that the God revealed in Jesus Christ is even now drawing all creation toward the fullness of God's creative intentions. In the midst of a now that tempts Christians to abandon this hope, J. Daniel Day makes a compelling case for a lively hope, in dialogue with the Bible's hopeful vision, a wide array of modern and contemporary hopers, and a world that makes hope truly an act of faith. I hope you will read it, and heed it!"

Steven R. Harmon
Professor of Historical Theology
Gardner-Webb University School of Divinity

"With his homespun stories, insightful research, and incredible wisdom, Dan Day offers us a taste of hope. You will laugh a bit, wipe a few tears, and find much to ponder in these pages. I'm indebted to Dan for his courage to point us again to the light of Hope that the darkness cannot overcome."

Bo Prosser
Catalytic Coach
Cooperative Baptist Fellowship

"I have been blessed on a personal level by reading *Lively Hope* and appreciate it enormously. Dan Day has done his biblical and theological homework, and has given us a solid book on hope that smart laypersons, who don't think they're theologians, can pick up and absorb. And he's had the courage to apply hope to America's current situation!"

Marv Knox
Coordinator
Fellowship Southwest

Lively Hope

A TASTE OF GOD'S TOMORROW

J. Daniel Day

© 2021
Published in the United
States by Nurturing Faith, Macon, GA.
Nurturing Faith is a book imprint of Good Faith Media (goodfaithmedia.org).
Library of Congress Cataloging-in-Publication Data is available.

ISBN: 978-1-63528-155-2

All scripture citations are from the New Revised International Version (NRSV)
unless otherwise indicated.

Contents

Acknowledgments

For early encouragement and suggestions for this book I am indebted to Bill Tillman and Fisher Humphreys. Another friend, Jim Travis, a pastoral care genius whose life and person inspire me as much as did his comments about hope, must be mentioned also. Ed Beddingfield and Daryll Powell provided helpful observations and coaching. Then there were some sessions with the Band of Brothers who pored over email attachments, helping me down the road. So did the Greater Raleigh Institute for Pastoral Expostulation, or GRIPE for short, whose members waded through first words and helped them become better words. If this book is a disappointment, don't blame these folks; they all tried, and I thank them.

My true appreciation is extended also to Hayes Barton Baptist Church of Raleigh, North Carolina, who permitted me to run some of this book's ideas by an adult Sunday School class during COVID-19 days—masked, distanced, and Zoomed. Above all, I want to note the great, good fortune that has been mine to have Mary Carol Rogers Day as a wife, friend, and cheerleader for more than five decades, and now a fifth book. That "good wife" whom Proverbs 31 has been trying to find for three thousand years? The one "who does her husband good, and not harm, all the days of her life"? I found her in the stairwell near the Snackery.

Two others surely must be thanked: Jackie Riley as the most patient editor in the whole world; and Vickie Frayne whose artistic skills conceived the cover and enhance every page of this book.

I dedicate this book to two groups of people. First, to those whose feelings are expressed by Cold Mountain's soul-battered soldier, Inman, who "had seen the metal face of the age and had been so stunned by it that when he thought into the future, all he could vision was a world from which everything he counted important had been banished or had willingly fled."[1] To you who look for hope, I dedicate these pages.

These pages are also dedicated to all who prop open the doors of hope. To you who, because of who you are and the way you live, are promise-material and imagination-igniters—to you who are hope-bearers even if you know it not, I dedicate these pages.

NOTE

[1]Charles Frazier, *Cold Mountain* (New York: Atlantic Monthly Press, 1997), 2.

Introduction

When Miss Ginny Watts of Nameless, Tennessee (pop. 90) ate "some bad ham meat," she described herself and condition as "hangin' on the drop edge of yonder."[1] I think I know that place. Maybe you do, too. But we didn't get there from trichinosis; we arrived by way of trying to digest current events.

It is true, of course, that many of the anxieties racing through us are not wed to current events or twenty-first-century novelties. Just as our ancestors did, we fear the "enemy" will come and conquer. We worry if there will be enough money. We lament the loss of good manners, certain the world is changing way too fast. We fret over our children. We avoid the doctor for fear she will tell us the worst. All of this is to say, apprehensions have always been nibbling at our peace, dangling us over "the drop edge."

But today feels different. Today we face an erosion of confidence in all the institutions that have historically provided our stability. Today we face the threat of global climate change and its societal impact, the ascendancy of "alternate facts" and the loss of "truth," the cumulative rage of four hundred years of unresolved racism, the growing percentage of us who identify religiously as "nones," the explosion of technologies that potentially make more of us feel "useless" and increasingly irrelevant—and these are just a few of the headliners. Carlos Caretto likened the 1970s to an astronaut hurtling through the cosmos at unimaginable speed in a technologically stunning space capsule—whose skin has already been fatally penetrated by a meteorite fragment.[2] For many people, that's the way it feels today.

Perhaps, as someone has suggested, it's not that things are getting worse: rather, they are just getting uncovered. Maybe so, but it certainly feels like something more has been dumped on us—or slipped inside us like some bad ham meat. A taste of it, distasteful as it might be, can be sampled by reviewing the covers of *Time* magazine during 2020. Here's a small selection, in chronological order, of the bold print theme-words on those covers:

The Fight for Equality
　When the World Stops
　　Finding Hope
　　　The Great Reckoning
　　　　The Overdue Awakening
　　　　　America Must Change

One Last Chance
The Plague Election
The New American Revolution
200,000: An American Failure
A Time to Heal
The COVID Winter
~~2020~~: The Worst Year Ever

Numerous historians are reconstructing how we got here. Honest and fairly presented historical research certainly helps us better understand the twists and turns of this and that moment of our journey. To a degree, historical studies can even suggest wise options. But history can carry us only so far. Crises arise in our personal and societal life when something more than information is essential. They are moments when what is within us meets dilemmas and demands that are beyond us, moments when we must choose hope or wilt in despair. Today feels like one of those moments. And this is a book about this moment and that choice. This is a book about hope.

But this is not an exhaustive treatise on hope. These are but meditations upon chosen aspects of hope about which I imagined I might say something helpful. In the process I discovered how difficult it is to speak realistically and honestly of hope. I struggled with how I might distinguish between our personal life-hopes and our hope for the world, finally concluding that as different as they may appear to be, they eventually meld into one. So, each meditation is an arrow aimed at a very large target. I "shoot" at hope as a life-force, as an anchor in time of trouble, as a socio-political dynamic, as a consolation in the presence of death, and more. Yet even in the aggregate, these meditations leave much unaddressed. My hope, however, is that I have "hit" a helpful midpoint between the devotional frothiness of some books on the subject and the academic impenetrability of others.

A note about the subtitle of this book may be of interest. *A Taste of God's Tomorrow* comes from a biblical description of Christians as those who have "tasted the powers of the age to come" (Heb. 6:5). The taste of death and deceit having become so pervasive among us, the flavor of hope may now seem as striking as a foreign spice. But I'd like to reintroduce it to our palate.

The book's main title, *Lively Hope* also comes from scripture, specifically from the venerable 1611 King James translation of 1 Peter 1:3, which says God has "begotten us again unto a lively hope." Those words appeared for four hundred years in the Authorized English Bible, but in those same four centuries, great gains were made in understanding the grammar and syntax of the New Testament's Greek, gains that began appearing in twentieth-century translations. One of the disliked gains was the introduction of the word "living" in place of the historic "lively" of 1 Peter 1:3. The new versions now spoke of a "living hope." Among the disturbed was an Anglican vestryman who sought an audience with his bishop. The conversation between the two of them went something like this:

"Your Lordship, this word 'living' just will not do," protested the vestryman. "It should be 'lively' just as it's always been!"

"And do you, sir, have expertise in the Greek language and purport to be a biblical linguist equal to those who have made these changes?"

"No sir. But everyone knows there's a big difference between 'living' and 'lively.' Why, take our vicar, for example. He's living, but he sure ain't lively!"[3]

The vestryman had his point. Even so, the scholars' "living" remained within the new translations; textual fidelity demanded it. But with the loss of "lively hope" a beautiful expression was lost.

My theme in this book is lively hope, because I know, as do you, that much in our society is "living" only by virtue of life-support mechanisms. I do not wish to linger by their bedsides, gawking at dying hopes. I want to explore lively hope, the kind that sings songs in the night and stares down long odds in clear daylight, the kind that dares to dance before the fiddler has even picked up his bow and won't stop talking until the right has been done. Anything less isn't worth your time or mine.

Although I have acknowledged historical information's limitations, I write with the conviction that the liveliest hope and the one that will sustain us best has deep roots in the soil of one unique strand of history. This particular past tells us about a childless Chaldean couple and their descendants. It reports an unwed pregnant teenager's holy yes. It ponders a crucified carpenter's life-giving death. These peoples' stories and the stories of their kinfolk lead us to "the God of hope" (Rom. 15:13), whose story is revealed within theirs. These stories form the nucleus of this book. I believe they have the power to lead us from "the drop edge of yonder" to "the confidence and the pride that belong to hope" (Heb. 3:6).

I am very aware, of course, that the hope I advocate is based upon a faith I cannot prove. What some people might dismissively call the "mythological" nature of my faith has been clear to me ever since childhood's naivete melted from beneath my feet decades ago. But these Christian "myths"—if myths they be—continue to amaze me by their depth and relevance. I have found no other river whose waters are as deep or as satisfying or as intellectually and emotionally powerful. Even if my beliefs were one day to be exposed as false, I would have no regrets for having held them. They have held me to the highest and served me too well to question their worthiness. Without reservation I pass them along to you, satisfied that "the fictions of God are truer than the facts of men."[4]

***

In the first section of this book, I attempt to provide a basis for understanding the phenomenon of hope. The meditations within this section are best read in the sequence printed, since each in some manner builds upon its predecessor. Although these six meditations are somewhat theoretical, I would urge readers to read them first for two reasons: Obviously, they provide a foundation for all that follows. But there is a second, very practical reason. Most every week of our life we have the opportunity to be an encourager of hope for others. But without some understanding of how hope "works," we are ill-prepared to be its allies. So, if you would be of help to others, see if my theory doesn't also provide some very practical guidance for doing it well.

In the second section I have offered meditations on various challenges hopers encounter. I hope at least a few of them scratch an itch you recognize. The final section deals with subjects usually discussed in books about hope. It would make sense, however, to have placed these meditations first, rather than last, because it is from our convictions about these "final" matters that everything else ultimately flows. Hope always begins at the end (and at the beginning), working its way into the now. Wherever you now are, I pray hope will work its way there—and soon.

NOTES

[1]William Least Heat Moon, *Blue Highways: A Journey into America* (New York: Fawcett Crest, 1982), 33.

[2]Carlo Caretto, *The God Who Comes* (Maryknoll, NY: Orbis Books, 1974), viii.

[3]I believe I first read this tale in Paul Rees' devotional study, *Triumphant in Trouble: Studies in First Peter* (Grand Rapids: Fleming Revell, 1962).

[4]Garrett Green, cited by Walter Brueggemann, *Finally Comes the Poet: Daring Speech for Proclamation* (Minneapolis: Fortress Press, 1989), 6.

PART 1
Foundations of Lively Hope

And the one who was seated on the throne said, "See, I am making all things new."
Also he said, "Write this, for these words are trustworthy and true."
Then he said to me, "It is done! I am the Alpha and the Omega,
the beginning and the end...."
(Rev. 21:5-6)

All my hope on God is founded,
who does still my trust renew.
Safe through change and chance God guides me,
ever faithful, ever true.
God unknown, God alone,
seeks to claim my heart as home.

Human pride and earthly glory,
sword and crown betray our trust;
though with care and toil we build them,
tower and temple fall to dust.
But God's power, hour by hour
is my temple and my tower.

But in every time and season,
out of love's abundant store,
God sustains the whole creation
fount of life forevermore.
We who share earth and air
count on God's unfailing care.

—Joachim Neander, 1680 (stanzas 1, 2)
—Fred Pratt Green, 1986 (stanza 3)

The Curious Cat with a Very Long Neck

I consider that the sufferings of this present time are not worth comparing with the glory about to be revealed to us. For the creation waits with eager longing for the revelation of the children of God....
(Rom. 8:18-19)

There once was a marmalade-colored Persian cat named Marmalade Apokaradokia. The cat's first name, the marmalade part, was easy enough to understand. All you had to do was look at its fur. But the *apokaradokia* part was tougher. To understand that you'd have to know the cat's owner who, in this case, happened to be a British-born minister with a better-than-average knowledge of the vocabulary of the Greek New Testament.

As the owner watched his cat walk through the house, the cat's neck always stretched to its full extent, his eyes slowly casting around, and his nose pointed up in curiosity—as though he was certain something was up, even if he hadn't identified it yet—this fellow thought of the Greek word *apokaradokia*. Bible translators have rendered the sense of the word as "being on tiptoe" and "waiting with eager expectation," but the British cleric saw it enacted every time his curious marmalade cat with a very long neck walked into the room.

According to the dictionaries, *apokaradokia* means "to watch with head erect or outstretched, to direct attention to anything, to wait for in suspense. It connotes constancy in expecting."[1] For the Apostle Paul, who uses it in Romans 8:19, it was the word for the posture of hope, for the full-stretched life eagerly looking for the magnificent future God has planned. It is the posture that makes life interesting and worth living.

Contrast it with the posture of the fellow on the cover of a national news magazine in 2020.[2] He was peering warily through partially-opened window blinds, looking upon a pandemic-emptied street in Paris, France. Or place *apokaradokia* next to the sprawled, pinned-to-the pavement black body of suffocating George Floyd. Or compare it with the rage of armed rioters racing through the United States Capitol, or the terror of Capitol employees hiding from them, crouching for hours behind and under tables in dark, locked rooms. These are samples of postures too frequently seen as I write, making me wonder what tomorrow's will be. No gift could be more welcome or more needed anytime than the confident posture that stands tall and walks unarmed and unafraid into each new day with curious expectancy.

That is also what God wants for us. When Jesus told us to pray, "Thy kingdom come, thy will be done on earth as it is in heaven," wasn't talking about pie-in-the-sky. He was telling us that the joy and freedom we associate with heaven isn't all tomorrow-talk. It is God's will for us to know it now, "on earth." He was saying something of heaven is truly possible here and now—not all of it, to be sure, but more of it than we are currently experiencing. God wants us to have a taste of tomorrow's wonder today. This is what that crazy cat's name is all about—walking around now, filled with enough hope to be eagerly on the lookout for the good that's still ahead.

In this book I talk about this hope, with sites from the Garden of Eden to the Pearly Gates being on the itinerary. But before we dive into all that, wet your feet by considering these hope-thoughts from various persons, nations, and eras:

Strong hope is a much greater stimulant of life than any single realized joy could be.[3]
—*Friedrich Wilhelm Nietzsche, German philosopher (1844–1900)*

Hope is the fundamental knowledge and feeling that there is a way out of difficulty, that things can work out, that we as human persons can somehow handle and manage internal and external reality, that there are "solutions"....[4]
—*William F. Lynch, American Jesuit priest, 1965*

The miserable have no other medicine/But only hope.[5]
—*William Shakespeare, British playwright (1564–1616)*

It's really a wonder that I haven't dropped all my ideals.... Yet I keep them, because in spite of everything I still believe that people are really good at heart. I simply can't build up my hopes on a foundation consisting of confusion, misery, and death. I see the world gradually being turned into a wilderness, I hear the ever-approaching thunder which will destroy us too, I can feel the sufferings of millions and yet, if I look up into the heavens, I think that it will all come right, that this cruelty too will end, and that peace and tranquility will return again. In the meantime, I must uphold my ideals, for perhaps the time will come when I shall be able to carry them out.[6]
—*Anne Frank, 14-year-old, attic-hidden, Jewish diarist, July 15, 1944*

Hope is a waking dream.[7]

—*Aristotle, Greek philosopher (384–322 BCE)*

Hope is for the soul what breathing is for the living organism. Where hope is lacking, the soul dries up and withers.[8]

—*Gabriel Marcel, French philosopher, 1962*

The lynching tree is a metaphor for white America's crucifixion of black people. It is the window that best reveals the religious meaning of the cross in our land… Just as Jesus had no choice in his journey to Calvary, so black people had no choice about being lynched. The evil forces of the Roman state and of white supremacy in America willed it. Yet, God took the evil of the cross and the lynching tree and transformed them both into the triumphant beauty of the divine. If America has the courage to confront the great sin and ongoing legacy of white supremacy with repentance and reparation there is hope "beyond tragedy."[9]

—*James H. Cone, American Black theologian, 2013*

Hope says to us constantly, "Go on, go on," and leads us to the grave.[10]

—*Francoise De Maintenon, Wife of Louis XIV of France (1635–1719)*

… [F]aith, wherever it develops into hope, causes not rest but unrest, not patience but impatience. It does not calm the unquiet heart, but is itself this unquiet heart in man. Those who hope in Christ can no longer put up with reality as it is, but begin to suffer under it, to contradict it. Peace with God means conflict with the world, for the goad of the promised future stabs inexorably into the flesh of every unfulfilled present.[11]

—*Jürgen Moltmann, German theologian, 1967*

All in all, then, maturing hope not only maintains itself in the face of changed facts—it proves itself able to change facts, even as faith is said to move mountains.[12]

—*Erik Erikson, German-American psychologist, 1964*

Hope is a very unruly emotion.[13]

—*Gloria Steinem, 20th-century American feminist*

Christian faith has always been teleological, believing that the creation is in process. History is going somewhere, en route to a destination, becoming something new. God is at work giving shape to the future and out in front of us calling us into this future… This understanding of God allows believers to adopt an anticipating consciousness that is energized by hope rather than deadened by despair.[14]

—*Andrew Lester, American pastoral counselor, 1995*

Lester's statement about God being out in front of us is likely not the location most of us would first designate. It's easier to imagine God "back then," as in the Bible stories, or "up there" on a heavenly throne. But God "out in front of us"? While that location may sound a bit different, it is as true as the others and it is a helpful way to begin to talk of hope. Think of it. Just as life and death come to and at us from the future, so does the God of life and death. The same psalm that assures us that God's "goodness and mercy shall follow me," also testifies that the Holy One is "with" us and will, like a good shepherd going in front of us, "lead" us. When God took on mortal flesh in the person of Jesus, the primary invitation was for his listeners to "follow" him into a way of life and unknown future, their one assurance being that he was going to be out there, in front, leading the way.

Now, if God is good and if God's tomorrow is half as good as preachers say, then answering the call to follow is sensible. But with Jesus' instruction to pray for heaven's ways to filter back into and become a part of "on earth," the terrain shifts. Now it's not just a matter of following Jesus to "there," but yearning for "there" to enter the here and now of my life and my society. So, what Jesus is calling us to is a life of opening earthly gates for an invasion today of God's tomorrow grandeur. God and all God's holy beauty and justice and peace are coming at us, and even the gates of hell cannot finally stop their entrance. But until then, the call is to live a life of hope, to a life of working and waiting for the splendor we are sure is ahead, for the invisible to become visible.

In the meditations that follow, I will develop this idea, exploring its roots and implications, and "test drive" it to see how it fares against tough thought and tougher life experiences. But for now, let me give the microphone to Howard Thurman, the always stimulating Black author, pastor, mystic, and soul guide.

In his little classic, *Jesus and the Disinherited*, Thurman illustrates Jesus' reverence for human personality by recalling the story of Jesus' defense of the woman taken in adultery (John 8). Though the woman was brought to Jesus in total humiliation, Jesus nonetheless honored her dignity by kneeling to write in the sand rather than staring at her. And, by banishing her accusers with his directive that "he that is without sin, let him first cast a stone," Jesus freed her from their condemnation and from his. He then spoke kindly to her, as a gracious friend. In all these ways he reawakened within her a dignity long dormant and, in Thurman's words, "he placed a crown over her head which for the rest of her life she would keep trying to grow tall enough to wear."[15]

Do you see this lady's stretched neck, her eagerness to see, now "free at last" from the torment of her life, what tomorrow might bring? That is *apokaradokia*, the posture of hope, the posture befitting those who, having been graced, now know that something amazing is underway. Rather than the "hang-dog" slump of the hopeless, this is the "heads-up" way hope looks.

NOTES

[1]Ernest T. Campbell, *Locked in a Room with Open Doors* (Waco, TX: Word Books, 1974), 63. The story of the cat is told in Campbell's sermon "More to Come," ibid., 55-63.

[2]*Time*, April 27/May 4, 2020.

[3]Cited in *21st Century Dictionary of Quotations*, ed. Princeton Language Institute (New York: Dell Publishing, 1993), 219.

[4]William F. Lynch, *Images of Hope: Imagination as Healer of the Hopeless* (Notre Dame, IN: University of Notre Dame Press, 1974), 32.

[5]William Shakespeare, *Measure for Measure*, in *The Riverside Shakespeare*, 2nd ed., edited by G. Blakemore Evans (Boston: Houghton Mifflin, 1997) 3.1.2-3.

[6]Anne Frank, *Anne Frank: The Diary of a Young Girl*, trans. B.M. Mooyaart-Doubleday (New York: Bantam, 1993), 263-264. Anne and her family were discovered by the Gestapo 20 days later, and Anne died in a German concentration camp that winter.

[7]Cited in 21st Century Dictionary of Quotations, 219.

[8]Gabriel Marcel, *Homo Viator: Introduction to a Metaphysics of Hope*, trans. Emma Crauford (New York: Harper & Row, 1962)

[9]James H. Cone, *The Cross and the Lynching Tree* (Maryknoll, NY: Orbis Books, 2013), 166

[10]Cited in 21st Century Dictionary of Quotations, 219.

[11]Jurgen Moltmann, *The Experiment Hope* (Cascade, OR: Wipf & Stock, 2003).

[12]Erik Erikson, *Insight and Responsibility* (New York: W.W. Norton Co., 1964), 117.

[13]Cited in Andrew Lester, *Hope in Pastoral Care and Counseling* (Louisville, KY: Westminster John Knox Press, 1995), 69.

[14]Ibid.

[15]Howard Thurman, *Jesus and the Disinherited* (Boston: Beacon Press, 1976), 96.

An Essential Dictionary Dive

Let the words of my mouth and the meditation of my heart be acceptable to you,
O LORD, my rock and my redeemer.
(Ps. 19:14)

The English language has more than a million words. Fortunately, many are scientific or technological terms and therefore aren't likely to be on your need-to-know list. Hope, however, is a need-to-know word, and I assume that it is within the 20,000+ words most college-educated Americans are said to have in their working vocabulary. Even so, some words we think we know well are more complex than imagined. The simple word "set," for instance, has 126 meanings as a verb, 58 as a noun, and 10 as a participial adjective. Our word "hope" isn't quite that complex, thank God, but it has its own quirks.

It can mean no more than a birthday wish, or as much as an Auschwitz prayer.

It can be used thoughtfully or innocuously, identifying a psychological mode or a town in Arkansas, or as a wave toward statistical probabilities.

You can deploy it as a noun—as Emily Dickinson famously did by dubbing hope "the thing with feathers"—or as a verb—as the fans in Miami do every spring, hoping this is the Marlins' year to win it all.

When a northbound peasant whispers it standing waist-deep in the Rio Grande, a solemnity greater than I can appreciate surrounds it, while the wonder in a mother's eyes as she views the newborn in her arms incarnates it in ways only another mother is likely to understand.

Voters will invariably garland the politician who promises the restoration of their hopes and, upon hearing of a "sure and certain hope," some graveside mourners find comfort.

To this very day, in some areas of the United States, "hope" is enunciated even when the clear intent is to speak of "help"—as in the question: "Can I 'hope' you, ma'am?" It's a regional mispronunciation, of course, but when you think about it, the best help you can give many times is the gift of hope.

So, to speak of hope is to name a palpable though invisible dynamic, an explosive amalgam of the essential, the holy, the commonplace, and the dangerous (because it is so very malleable).

This complexity of hope's meanings is present within the Bible as well. Without doubt the word is used in everyday, commonplace ways in the Old

Testament. But when we study its significant theological uses, two nuances are evident. It is often used to signify a trustful waiting upon God to act, as in Psalm 130:5—"I wait for the LORD, my soul waits, and in his word I hope." Toward the latter part of the Old Testament, however, the word sometimes carries a more specific focus, pointing to an anticipated event, a good time coming for the people of Israel. Jeremiah 31:16-17 provides a sample of this: "Keep your voice from weeping, and your eyes from tears…, there is hope for your future, says the LORD: your children shall come back to their own country." So, the first testament speaks of hope as both an action and as a longed-for event. But both uses share the characteristic of suspense. Something isn't yet complete, and in both uses God is the one being looked to for that completion. Within the Old Testament, then, hope was understood as an expression of trust in God's fidelity and goodness.

These same understandings are carried forward into the New Testament, albeit somewhat reshaped by the coming of Jesus. Most importantly, hope is reshaped by the astonishing resurrection of Jesus Christ from the dead. Apart from this event the followers of Jesus would have had no distinct "hope" to cherish or to herald; after all, their supposed Messiah had been executed. It was the Resurrection that saved them from being everyone's laughing stock. But much more important, it was the Resurrection that emphatically said something stupendous about God.

In God's act of raising Jesus from the dead, God demonstrated that God had not withdrawn from this world; that God could still act to vindicate the good and right and holy; that evil did not always have the last word. In short, the Resurrection gave to these first believers the assurance that there really was reason to hope in God. The God their ancestors had waited for and hoped in had acted once again. No wonder their writings in multiple ways throb with the conviction that God truly had given them "a new birth into a living hope through the resurrection of Jesus Christ from the dead" (1 Pet. 1:3). God was still in business!

Strangely, this resurrection emphasis has led some interpreters to the odd conclusion that the only kind of hope Christians can legitimately talk about is otherworldly or religious hope. They say that Christian hope has to do only with things such as Jesus' second coming, our death, resurrection, heaven, and the world to come. Without digging too long into theology books, you can even find comments like this: "The New Testament conception of hope has nothing at all to do with any this-worldly prospects; it is as far removed as possible from any notion of an earthly Utopia or any secular optimism. It is through and through eschatological, always bearing reference to the return of the LORD Jesus at the end of the age."[1]

This kind of conclusion, however, actually robs us of hope. If Jesus' resurrection deals only with next-life issues, our daily life and earthly world are left little better. However, precisely because Jesus' resurrection from the dead is the upending of the material limits and power relations we know in life, there is no corner of creation or dimension of life that is not affected by it. What it says about Who has the upper hand in history must not be railroaded off just to "tomorrow" subjects such as heaven and the world to come. If, by the will and power of a compassionate God, Jesus lives and his Spirit is still active among us, then we have grounds for hope in this life, and upon this earth—as well as hope for a future life in a world to come. If the Resurrection is a fact, it is a game-changer for what we can say about hope, and what we can legitimately hope for.

Because Jesus lives, the single mother of three children in a fourth-floor walk-up on Chicago's southside has resurrection reason to hope her kids won't forever be damned to their present.

Because Jesus lives, the teenager who's been hooked on opioids since he was eleven years old has resurrection reason to hope for a drug-free tomorrow.

Because Jesus lives, the elderly couple down the hall has resurrection reason to hope death will not have the final word on their lives.

Because Jesus lives, the marchers for racial equity have resurrection reason to hope their pounding the pavement will make a difference.

Hope is not just for the next world. It is for the whole world, now. Jesus' resurrection shouts that a resurrecting God, a caring God, must not be ruled out of any scene, regardless of how apparently hopeless.

But when we speak of this hope, we are wise to distinguish it from optimism. (Not that optimism is bad—not at all. I'd be "outta here" if I had to live among a nest of pessimists!) Although hope and optimism are often conflated—and I am sure old habits of equating the two will inevitably appear in these pages—I would suggest that we at least attempt to separate the two. That separation might at times seem as porous as the separation between church and state, but these separations serve helpful analytic purposes. I can, for example, be full of hope but not be very optimistic!

I understand optimism to be dealing with the immediate future, and I understand hope to be dealing with the longer perspective. If this is so, I might have little optimism that better race relations will be evident soon, but also be very hopeful that eventually "we shall overcome." Or, as another example, my doctor may give me no reason to be optimistic that any therapies will defeat my cancer, but I can still live bravely because my hope anticipates a healing that will be eternal.

An extension of this explanation is to define optimism as a sunny emotional outlook based on data that may be interpreted positively or negatively—the glass half empty/half full scenario. Optimism comes from projecting positive outcomes onto this scene, grounding those projections on presently observable trends. Hope, in contrast, looks at the visible and even peers into the invisible and, seeing nothing encouraging, nonetheless walks with head erect into a future held in God's kind hands. Hope anchors itself in the conviction that the future belongs to God and that goodness therefore will win—somehow, someday. Staring into an ugly existential abyss that will swallow optimism in a single, easy gulp, hope still dares to say confidently, "Nonetheless!" Or, as one preacher summed it up: "Today may be dark; tomorrow may be even darker. But God owns the day after tomorrow."[2]

A final way of distinguishing these two is to suggest that optimism may be only a feeling, a mood of positivity. Perhaps it comes from a genetic predisposition or an unnicked life or just a good lunch. Hope, on the other hand, is a cry, a shout, a reaching out for more. Optimism splashes about in the kiddie pool, whereas hope swims in deep water. The eight verses of Psalm 130 actually provide this picture of hope's truest habitat.

In the interior verses of Psalm 130, we hear the author's testimony: "I wait for the LORD, my soul waits, and in his word I hope." This testimony builds toward the psalm's concluding plea: "O Israel, hope in the LORD! For with the LORD there is steadfast love, and with him is great power to redeem." But the opening words of the psalm reveal the situation that has prompted this outburst of hope-talk. The psalm begins with this plea: "Out of the depths I cry to you, O LORD. LORD, hear my voice!" Hope, in biblical perspective, is always in over its head and calling out from the depths, seeking the improbable. Hope, then, is more than a chipper attitude; it is a chosen behavior that moves toward a better tomorrow, daring to risk and invest itself in the invisible.

So, what have I tried to say in this dictionary dive? I have tried to say that words matter, and most certainly words matter when one of the words is hope. I have tried to say that within the Bible the word "hope" points to God, and to God's power and surprising faithfulness—not to happy talk and easy optimism. I have tried to say that hope, like everything else about God, has a mysterious, desperate grandeur to it.

NOTES

[1] Alan Richardson, "Hope," in *A Theological Word Book of the Bible*, Alan Richardson, ed. (New York: Macmillan, 1962), 109.

[2] A friend recalls the phrase from a chapel sermon delivered by William E. Hull at Southern Baptist Theological Seminary in Louisville, Ky. The complete thought is found in Hull's *Harbingers of Hope* (Birmingham, AL: Samford University Press, 2007), 248.

In the Beginning, Hope

In the beginning when God created the heavens and the earth, the earth was a formless void and darkness covered the face of the deep, while a wind from God swept over the face of the waters. Then God said, "Let there be light"; and there was light. And God saw that the light was good; and God separated the light from the darkness. God called the light Day; and the darkness he called Night. And there was evening and there was morning, the first day.
(Gen. 1:1-5)

A friend of mine often summarized his day by saying, "I just spent another of my Tuesdays returning phone calls." I found his way of speaking quaint—and sobering. We have only so many Tuesdays before our supply runs out.

This sense of time, this feeling of a clock counting down an allotment of hours, this ability to remember yesterday and anticipate tomorrow—the human animal is presumably the only species that knows of this. But you and I do perceive ourselves as finite creatures moving from infancy to adulthood toward an unyielding conclusion. And somewhere along the way, time-related emotions become a part of our journey. Regrets about yesterday and anxieties about tomorrow arise. The permanence of our past and the mystery of our future become major players. This is so, whether we are six-year-olds waiting for Christmas or incontinent octogenarians entering hospice care or Syrian refugees searching for a home. What was and is and is yet to come shapes us.

Curiously, within each of us there also seems to be a default setting called hope. Visions of better, happier days lure us onward. Even in the bleakest of circumstances, a gritty defiance of the unwanted bubbles up from within. I'm told that extensive psychological testing documents an "optimism bias" within us so pronounced that expressions such as "incurable optimist" and "hope springs eternal" become most credible. How else can we explain cheerful smiles in a children's cancer ward or divorcees risking a third "I do"? How else can we interpret sports fans buying season tickets for teams that haven't broken .500 since Jackie Robinson suited up for the Brooklyn Dodgers? We do seem to be hardwired to "look on the sunny side of life."

I am, of course, profoundly grateful that a can-do spirit does arise within us; I don't want to contemplate a world that has no dreamers or where bad news is uniformly met with resignation and submission. In 1992 P.D. James published a bone-chilling novel (set in 2021!) about precisely that kind of world. She wrote of life on Earth twenty-five years after the last human being had been born. The main character summarizes the situation:

> The world didn't give up hope until the generation born in 1995
> reached sexual maturity. But when the testing was complete and
> not one of them could produce fertile sperm, we knew this was
> the end of Homo sapiens. It was in that year, 2008, that the
> suicides increased... In our hearts few of us believe that the cry of a
> newborn child will ever be heard again on our planet.[1]

Such a despairing, futureless world is ghastly to contemplate. Even if we are guilty of being incurable optimists, our persistent hopefulness is immeasurably better than the rule of despair. But this only raises a most basic question: Where does all this hope come from?

The quick answer is that hope is built into the human psyche—that we truly are hopers by nature. While I would not disagree with that reply, I believe it quits too soon. Hope is much more than a "natural" reflex, a peristaltic push of adrenal happy-thoughts to help us handle the challenges of life. Hope is a rescuing wonder of the human person. Behind every admirable achievement of humankind and of every individual there is the encouraging face of hope. Hope lifts us, hope motivates us, hope saves us.

I would propose that a better answer for the origin of hope is to attribute it to nature's God. Hope is an expression of God's compassion embedded within the very structure of the world. This, at least, is the way the Genesis accounts of creation tell the story.

Those stories say that as soon as light had been summoned to appear in the darkness, God separated the two and called the light Day and the darkness Night. "And there was evening and there was morning, the first day" (1:5). Notice the order: God's primal action was to move from evening to morning, from darkness to light. The Creator begins the unfolding of the universe with the displacement of darkness by light, by pushing the story forward—toward the dawn.

From day one, the God of the Bible relentlessly pushes each day and all things toward the dawn. This is the Creator's repetitious rhythm. The creation text speaks only of seven days—a perfect number—but after those seven dawns, the pattern is established and the creature may assume that God's "darkness to dawn" movement carries a promise, an assurance of a tomorrow. Whatever the darkness of any hour, it won't be night always!

These ancient storytellers were not astrophysicists nor witnesses to the creation event they report. But I am persuaded they told the story the way they did, not because they were scientific know-nothings, but because they found spiritual resonance within it. The darkness-to-dawn movement paralleled their happiest life stories. "Out of the depths" of life they had cried for God's help, saying: "I wait for the LORD, my soul waits, and in his word I hope; my soul waits for the LORD more than those who watch for the morning, more than those who watch for the morning" (Ps. 130: 1, 5-6). Why this eagerness for the morning? Because "weeping may linger for the night, but joy comes with the morning" (Ps. 30:5). Or, as one prophet put it: "The LORD's appearing is as sure as the dawn; he will come to us like the showers, like the spring rains that water the earth" (Hos. 6:3). A Christian leader later appeals to this same associative dynamic when (1 Pet. 4:19) he urges suffering Christians to "entrust themselves to a faithful Creator"—that is, to the Dawn Bringer, the God of hope.

Long before anyone knew about a heliocentric solar system and its planetary orbits and shadows, the Hebrews were saying this world was created with tomorrows included. A psychic, rescuing affect was lodged within this geophysical phenomenon. I first experienced this when my newborn twin sons were hospitalized for respiratory failure. They were so frightfully small—I could hold both in my palms like tiny loaves of bread—and so very fragile. In the deepest hours of one long night, I walked from the glare of hospital corridors to the far corner of a parking lot, searching for the solace of darkness. And there I wept, gripped by fear, and prayed as never before or since for dawn, for one more day in which my little boys' lungs might grow stronger.

It is a story, a hope known by all who endure all-night vigils aching for one more day, or who long for justice in an unjust world, or who seek relief from smothering grief. Maureen McGovern's hope-filled song, "The Morning After," from the Vietnam/Watergate era continues to say it well:

There's got to be a morning after
If we can hold on through the night
We have a chance to find the sunshine
Let's keep on lookin' for the light.

Oh, can't you see the morning after
It's waiting right outside the storm
Why don't we cross the bridge together
And find a place that's safe and warm?

It's not too late, we should be giving,
Only with love can we climb
It's not too late, not while we're living
Let's put our hands out in time.

There's got to be a morning after
We're moving closer to the shore
I know we'll be there by tomorrow
And we'll escape the darkness
We won't be searching any more.[2]

In addition to this dawn-movement, the gift of plants and seeds speaks of an orderly world where sowing and harvesting and expectant waiting are within life's structure. Even when Adam/Eve tragically "blow it" and are expelled from the garden, the door of the future is not closed. God speaks to them of children and of work to be done. To their murderous son Cain, God grants the gift of a protected future (Gen. 4:15), and the Noah story ends with a rainbow memorial as a pledge of "seedtime and harvest," a promise that "summer and winter, day and night shall not cease" (8:20-22).

The creation stories even leave open the door for a continuing creation. The pronouncement following each day, that its work was "good," does not mean it was finished and complete. Rather, that verdict speaks of the goodness, of the "just rightness" of what God has done and perhaps even that it was now "good to go" for the next stage of creating. Creation is not a closed system, a past-tense deed. God is still creating! God's universe is open to the "new," and straining forward, awaiting whatever still remains up God's sleeve. Paul writes: "The whole creation [is] groaning in labor pains" (Rom. 8:22), pushing toward some tomorrow, some "more" that is pending.

In sum, we live in a dependably dawn-oriented world that is ripe with promise and futurity. Every daybreak, season, and living thing can whisper tomorrow to those whose ears are open.[3] I am admittedly getting ahead of myself here, but Christian readers may already have recalled that the open tomb of Jesus wasn't discovered on a Sunday afternoon stroll, but "on the first day of the week, at early dawn" (Luke 24:1).

I like to think of this world—childishly, no doubt—as a marvelous sandbox for God's children to play in. It is a bounteous place with dependable, strong walls to hold us all—a place well-suited to us.

But that does not mean it is without danger. Ugly things happen—even in sandboxes—things that can break our hearts and make us angry with the place, its inhabitants, and its Maker. Writing from the Black experience in America, Langston Hughes voiced this when he wondered, "What happens to a dream deferred?" He asks if it dries up like a raisin in the sun, or begins to stink like rotten meat, or sag like a heavy load, "or does it explode?"[4] Explosions can happen even in sandboxes and can leave us deaf to tomorrow's promise.

Still, the walls of the sandbox hold firm. The world does not explode even if we and our dreams do. Regardless of how we feel, tomorrow happens and with it, the gift of possibility. As one surprised sufferer discovered: "The steadfast love of the LORD never ceases, his mercies… are new every morning" (Lam. 3:22-23). But we must be honest here. These "new mercies" do not include a full-blown, ready-to-use suitcase full of hope. Rather, among the debris from our broken dreams a merciful God deposits the hammer and nails and glue of hope. Amid the fragments are the ingredients of hope.

The story of Chuck Noland, a FedEx employee abandoned for four years on a deserted island, is told in the 2000 movie *Cast Away*. His forsaken, lonely years finally end when Noland successfully cobbles together a raft that carries him out to the shipping lanes where a freighter rescues him. A few days later, in a FedEx conference room in Memphis, Noland recounts his experience to a friend.

He begins by telling of his total despair when, after a failed suicide, he realized he "couldn't even kill myself the way I wanted to. I had power over nothing." Yet, that's when he says a feeling came over him, telling him that he had to stay alive: "Somehow, I had to keep breathing. Even though there was no reason to hope." And that is precisely what Noland did.

Though all his logic said he would never see Memphis again, "I kept breathing. And one day my logic was proven all wrong because the tide came in and gave me a sail. And now, here I am. I'm back. In Memphis, talking to you." Then, with a final resolve, he who has lost not only four years but also the love of his life during his castaway hell, declares: "And I know what I have to do now. I gotta keep breathing. Because tomorrow the sun will rise. Who knows what the tide could bring?"[5]

The promise of tomorrow and another dawn, the possibility of a favorable tide—as bare as they were, for Chuck Noland these were the hammer and nails and glue of hope. There are others. In the next meditations I will name some of them.

NOTES

[1] P.D. James, *The Children of Men* (New York: Alfred A. Knopf, 1992), 7, 8.

[2] Al Kasha and Joel Hirschhorn, "The Morning After," 1972. Copyright believed to be owned by WC Music Corp and Warner-Tamerlane Pub Corp. No response received to permission request.

[3] Even the Old Testament prophets, often thought to be only doomsday scolds, are ultimately voices of hope. A growing consensus of scholars say that by their placement within the canon and by their contents, the "major prophets" (Isaiah, Jeremiah, Ezekiel) and the 12 "minor" prophets (Hosea through Malachi) all move "from utterance of judgment to utterance of hope." See Walter Brueggemann, *From Judgment to Hope* (Louisville, KY: Westminster John Knox, 2019), x.

[4] Langston Hughes, "Dream Deferred" ("Harlem"), from *The Panther and the Lash* (New York: Alfred A. Knopf, 1951).

[5] *Cast Away*, 20th Century Fox Films, 2000: Screenwriter William Broyles, Jr.

Promises and Other Odd Fathers

Now the LORD *said to Abram, "Go from your country and your kindred and your father's house to the land that I will show you. I will make of you a great nation, and I will bless you, and make your name great, so that you will be a blessing. I will bless those who bless you, and the one who curses you I will curse; and in you all the families of the earth shall be blessed."*
(Gen. 12:1-3)

The Bible is often dubbed the Good Book. But excerpting the first two chapters (where God is the only actor), the next nine chapters are certifiably depressing. In them you read of Adam and Eve getting kicked out of a lavishly beautiful garden (and of a talking snake that's somewhat to blame for this), of one of their sons murdering his brother over "religious practices," of a flood that wipes the whole creation clean—except for a drunken survivor and his family—and of a high-rise building project that goes disastrously awry. It's a grim collection of stories supposedly told to "explain" how and why things are as they are.

But by the time you come in sight of Genesis 12, you have to wonder how long "things as they are" can last. The world is now alienated from its Creator, lacerated by far more than seven deadly sins, and hamstrung by the peoples' inability even to talk with one another since every group knows only its own language. Unless something very different enters this story soon, Management needs to pull the plug.

Fortunately, that "something different" enters the story precisely at this moment. Genesis 12 begins with the Creator speaking to a Chaldean by the name of Abram, making the hope-introducing promise printed in verses 1-3. The "something different" now on stage is a God who makes promises. Biblical scholar Walter Brueggemann says that of all the bold things said in the Old Testament about God, the claim that God makes promises is Israel's "oddest testimony."[1] Not least of all, it is odd in its latent invitation to every reader of the Bible to see if the God of Israel, known by the name of YHWH, is actually going to be able to make good on this Genesis 12 promise to bring blessing into our global devastation.

Be sure to note, then, that in this promise YHWH announces an intent to bless not just Abram's lineage but "all the families of the earth." Whatever YHWH is up to, it is certainly more than being just a tribal deity (the God of the Israelites). This then means you and I, as downstream participants in this "all," are somehow figured into this story. Moreover, if YHWH is going to bless all of us, the inference is that all this world, all its people, and all its history are within God's power.

Today we hem and haw about how much influence God actually has within the affairs of this world, but in this promise, God's orchestrating powers are both claimed and put on the table for anyone to judge. There *is* an oddness here! And in this jaw-dropping promise, the ground for hope deepens and expands far beyond God's creation assurances of a tomorrow (see "In the Beginning, Hope").

Whatever happens from this moment on, a divine promise now hovers over the human story. A holy purpose of blessing is to be at work by One who is no indifferent observer or powerless bystander. On an ominously darkened world stage, a beam of fascinating light now shines. For the One who said, "Let there be light," now promises all the families of the earth: "I will be working for your blessing." And this is pledged, in spite of the garbage pail the human has already made of God's creation!

In this story we see a bedrock foundation for our understanding of hope: God's promises rest at the heart of hope. They form the backdrop for all its other expressions. For if there is a God with global blessing as the declared purpose of the human story, then we have a basis for hoping that the rest of the story—including our own—will be better than that depressing anthology in Genesis 1–11. The promises of God provide the soil in which all our hopes may grow.

Another way of saying this is to say that hope arises from faith, from trust in the promises of God. This is so not only with this primal promise of a blessing-purpose being worked out in history, but it is also the case with regard to all other expressions of Christian hope. For instance, when Christians speak of the forgiveness of sins they speak as hopers in the promise of divine forgiveness. We have no demonstrable "proof" of divine forgiveness; it remains a cherished hope because of biblical words of promise that have elicited our faith. Similarly, when Christians speak of resurrection and of life beyond this mortal one, we are speaking as hopers in the non-demonstrable truth of certain words of promise about being raised up into new life. Hope arises from faith in the promises of God.

Eighteenth-century slave trader turned Anglican minister, John Newton, saw the connection between God's promise and our hope and wrote of it as one expression of God's "Amazing Grace." In a too-seldom sung stanza of his now-famous hymn, there is this:

The LORD has *promised* good to me,
His word my hope secures;
He will my shield and portion be
As long as life endures.

He then paired this theological profession with a corroborating testimony:

Through many dangers, toils, and snares,
I have already come;
'Tis grace hath brought me safe thus far,
And grace will lead me home.

Although we know this hymn as "Amazing Grace," it's also a song about hope, about hope that came and comes as a gift of God's grace through the promises of God.[2]

It might be helpful for us to attempt to see this pairing as the ancient Israelites did. Though we typically think of the future as being "before" us, they apparently saw it differently. In their way of thinking, they were walking backward into the future, because the only thing they could clearly see was the past. The future was hidden from view. But by reckoning from what God had done in the past, Israel could hope to navigate the unseeable future well.[3] Remembering the past, recalling promises kept, hope found rootage. It is for this reason that we find repeated calls within the Old Testament and within today's Judaism to "remember."

Christian faith shares much of this mindset of memory funding hope. For us, too, the scaffolding of hope is built upon yesterday. As one example, note the words "In Remembrance of Me" etched across thousands of Christian communion tables and altars. In the bread and wine resting upon them, these tables hold the church's memories of a life given and a deed done for the world. And through the "in remembrance" phrase, spoken by Jesus in and for the darkest of hours, Christians remember where our ultimate hope begins. To be sure, Christian hope also has a future orientation and horizon, and I'll speak of that later, but even that tomorrow rests on this historical base. We take our bearings from what has been. "In remembrance" we move from darkness to dawn.

I cannot overstate the significance of promises, of records and memories of past good, as the basis for the emergence of hope. God's record as a promise-keeping God is the backdrop for all our lesser hopes. It is the ultimate frame of reference for how we might come to hope for any other good and beautiful thing to happen in this life. God's promise of a blessing-purpose for this world—this is a foundation for our hope.

But God is not so self-centered, so narrow, as to confine the phenomenon of hope within a Judeo-Christian tradition. Within God's blessing-purpose there is "plenty good room" for other portals to hope, but each one of them is characterized by the promised qualities of fidelity, dependability, and blessing. Some of these "promises" are so scant you can barely call them promises.

The surgeon says, "I think we got all of the tumor"—and on the surgeon's "I think," hopes are built. Or a mother calms a frightened child by promising, "It's going to be okay!"—and with those words the child's fear dissipates. When we ask ourselves why these utterances have such effect, the reason is not difficult to discern. The surgeon's "I think" has proven to be correct in many past occasions—and so we hope. The mother who promises "It's going to be okay" has been reliable in the past—and so the child hopes. Even Little Orphan Annie sings confidently about "Tomorrow," and is so certain you can "bet your bottom dollar the sun'll come out tomorrow," because it always has. Hope, in myriad ways, is a matter of standing (and sometimes hanging, even dangling!) on promises, on memories of past good.

A friend of mine understands this through the prism of the promise some adults saw in him when he was still a struggling adolescent. They saw promise where he saw nothing but the elbows and awkwardness of teenage confusion. Yet their vision was enough to propel him forward to a gratifying life and, in his telling of it, their vision continues to guide him as a midlife adult.

A promise does so much! It creates expectations, invites trust, and often introduces an eagerness to turn the next page. Promises provide the foundation of hope, whether they be the promises of God or what I call the "promise-material" provided through the example or words of parents, family members, doctors, teachers, coaches, and friends. Whoever proves themselves to be dependable, good, and affirming forces in our lives, these are promise-material.

And what about those who have had little or no experience of such steadfastness, people for whom memory "can carry [you] through some dark rooms where the walls seem lined with razor blades"?[4] It is the responsibility of those with better histories to live trustworthily before them so that they might find promise-material in us—an experience or memory of admirable character to build upon. And it is the privilege of those with hope in God to tell them of a trustworthy God so that an even higher hope might find them.

For when yesterday and its promises have been forgotten or erased—or are pockmarked by cruelty—hope has no foundation from which to rise.

My Dad's father died when my Dad was still in grade school. The Great Depression fell only months after Dad finished high school, and so he finished only one semester of college before his financially-stricken family called him home. He never returned to school. He went to work: at a grocery store, for an insurance company, then running a city's bus line, a drugstore, a farm machinery business, and twenty-five years serving as a pastor for a string of churches that broke his heart—and Mom's—a dozen times. As he entered his nineties, and some ailment demanded he see a doctor, a puzzled radiologist asked him: "When did you break your neck?" What? None of us knew of any such thing, but it finally explained why night after night during my childhood years the house had to become as quiet as a funeral parlor because Dad had come home with another splitting headache. Through it all, broken neck or broken heart, Dad remained as steady as Gibraltar, a man to admire and to trust.

Though he never was one for gushy talk, his hopes for me and the hopes he nurtured in me were real, and more costly to him than I knew. I understood this better, though, when I was nearly thirty and finishing a second graduate degree. I sat one day at his desk and discovered a poem he'd copied by hand decades earlier and had slipped under the desktop's glass covering:

I walked a mile with Pleasure;
She chatted all the way;
But left me none the wiser
For all she had to say.

I walked a mile with Sorrow
And ne'er a word said she,
But, oh! the things I learned from her,
When Sorrow walked with me.[5]

We wonder sometimes how we might increase the inventory of hope within our wearied world. A powerful but overlooked method is the practice of fidelity. To be a keeper of promises, a person of dependability, a witness to God's fidelity, a depositor of good memories, is to be a father of hope.

And when, perchance, the candle of our own hope flickers, its flame can be rekindled by memories of the promise-keepers in our life—and by remembering the Ultimate Promiser.

But now thus says the LORD, he who created you, O Jacob, he who formed you, O Israel: Do not fear, for I have redeemed you; I have called you by name, you are mine. When you pass through the waters, I will be with you; and through the rivers, they shall not overwhelm you; when you walk through fire you shall not be burned, and the flame shall not consume you. For I am the LORD your God, the Holy One of Israel, your Savior. (Isa. 43:1-2)

NOTES

[1] Walter Brueggemann, *Theology of the Old Testament: Testimony, Dispute, Advocacy* (Minneapolis: Fortress Press, 1995), 164-173.

[2] Newton's title for his poem was "Faith's Review and Expectation."

[3] Hans Walter Wolff, *Anthropology of the Old Testament* (Philadelphia: Fortress Press, 1974), 88.

[4] Rick Bragg, *All Over But the Shoutin'* (New York: Pantheon Books, 1997), xiii.

[5] Robert Browning Hamilton, "Along the Road."

The Eyes of Your Heart

I pray that the God of our Lord *Jesus Christ, the Father of glory, may give*
you a spirit of wisdom and revelation as you come to know him, so that,
with the eyes of your heart enlightened, you may know what is the hope to
which he has called you, what are the riches of his glorious inheritance among
the saints, and what is the immeasurable greatness of his power for us who
believe....

(Eph. 1:15-19)

If you are thumbing through the Bible looking for something to bolster your
hope, Ecclesiastes isn't the destination I would choose. It's a fairly depressing
neighborhood. Among other things, Ecclesiastes contends that the rhythms
of nature and their implied tomorrows, which I find so hopeful, are not so
hope-filled after all. They only demonstrate the dreary, unrelieved drumbeat
of sameness.

The author agrees that "the sun rises," but then adds that "the sun [also]
goes down, and hurries to the place where it rises" (1:15) just to do it again
and again—but nothing ever really changes! The verdict? "All things are
wearisome.... What has been is what will be, and what has been done is what
will be done; there is nothing new under the sun" (1:8-9). If we are hardwired
with at least the capacity to hope, Ecclesiastes' circuitry has come apart. Life
is not tomorrow-oriented for Ecclesiastes.

Still, even from Ecclesiastes' dissent, there is an important lesson about
hope to be learned. If we make too much of nature's steady repetitions, it can
lead to a deadening, cyclical understanding of history. The dawning of a new
day, then, does not signify another opportunity but only another revolution
of the merry-go-round.

To be sure, you can amuse yourself to death on this merry-go-round—the
painted ponies do pump up and down, the canned music plays, the people come
and go and giggle and grin—but the contraption itself never goes anywhere.
Indeed, there is no place for it to go; it's just a mindless machine that someday
will wheeze and whimper to its clatter-bang conclusion. Any rosy notion about
the wonder of another day and its hope is a cruel deception, for tomorrow is
ultimately a burden to be borne rather than a gift to be welcomed.

This is not an unheard-of stance. Many people are driven to it. In the early
days of World War II, Felix Sparks was a young lieutenant in the U.S. Army. By
the war's end he had led troops of the 45th Infantry Division through bloody

battles in Sicily, Italy, France, and Germany, finally serving as their commanding officer.

In a TV miniseries dramatizing those years, a war-weary Sparks writes his wife, admitting: "I need to feel what hope feels like again...and soon!"[1] He has seen too much daily death, with little changing other than the location of the killing fields. Unfortunately, his yearning for hope comes just before his troops come upon Dachau, forcing him to inhale the stench of its piled-high, decomposing bodies and view its thousands of emaciated prisoners. Decades later, he wrote of that event and concluded with these words:

> Dachau was but one of the many monuments left behind by depraved and tyrannical ruling individuals and groups of the past. As I recall, we were often told during the course of World War II that we were fighting a war to end all wars. As I view the world scene today, it seems that very little has changed since the end of the war. In the name of nationalism, religion, political affiliation, greed, racial superiority, economics, or varied combinations thereof, innocent people around the world are still being killed, kidnapped, or brutalized on a daily basis. And so it shall ever be.[2]

Or, as Ecclesiastes says: "What has been is what shall be...there is nothing new under the sun."

If hope is to be anything more than sweet sentimentality, if it is to have enough substance to stand against the forlorn faces and facts of perpetual brutality, something more is needed than sunrises and moonbeams—and even promises. That ingredient is imagination.[3]

Return to the concept of promises and look again at YHWH's promises to Abram. But this time, pay attention to the content of what is promised—and the legitimate questions Abram might have raised.

God promises: A land that I will show you.
   Okay, but will it be mountainous, seaside, desert, pastures, or what?
God promises: I will make of you a great nation.
   Great, but how? Financially? Militarily? Culturally? Or all of the above?
God promises: I will bless you.
   Can you tell me more about what it means to be "blessed" by you?
God promises: I will make your name great.
   Will that be in my lifetime or later? And what qualifies as "great"?

God promises: You will be a blessing.
  Ditto to earlier question about blessing.
God promises: In you all the families of the earth shall be blessed.
  How on earth could that ever happen?

This fictional dialogue underscores how poetically alluring and yet how mystifyingly unspecific the promises are. They are huge but lack detail. YHWH speaks in generalities, not in footnotes; in promises, not in contracts. No documents are signed allowing Abram later to sue over the fine print. God's speech is wholly relational. "You have my word on it: trust me!" The consequence of this is that God's promises provoke questions. They arouse curiosity, a curiosity that then looks to imagination to fill in the blanks.

Promises provide only the groundwork for hope, not the thing itself. To become energizing hope, promises need the touch of imagination. When imagination begins to play with the promise, be intrigued by it, meditate upon it, pick it up and visualize what the promise might mean, then hope has been conceived. And when this synergy results in acts or attitudes of expectancy, hope has been born.

Suppose a father tells his daughter at breakfast time that he has a surprise for her tonight. She knows him to be a man of his word, so she has no doubt he will return tonight with the promised surprise. But what will it be? When her curiosity kicks into gear, and her imagination begins to play with the promise, then the promise becomes a tantalizing hope. She envisions a puppy, or a sweater, or a trip to a favorite amusement park. But more than any specific item of desire, her entire day becomes energized and illumined by the expectation that soon she will experience something good. The combination of promise and imagination has created an entire day of vibrant hope for this little girl.

In a similar way the promises of God can elicit curiosity and wonderment within us—or, of course, we can ignore them and remain unaltered. But when we turn our full attention to those promises, and permit our imagination to interrogate them, hope can begin to germinate. It comes to fullness when imagination gives way to action based on the promise. That action may be as quiet as an altered attitude toward the day or as public as a protest before a city council meeting. In Abraham's case, hope was full-blown when he packed his bags and struck out for God's Somewhere.

Consider how this is presented in the longest—and arguably the least exciting—psalm in the Bible: Psalm 119. In a seemingly endless flow of verses

(176 total), we hear two themes: praise for the Torah's instruction and stout professions of love for every word of it. After the umpteenth declaration of these themes, many of us are wishing this psalmist had had a better editor!

However, another way to hear this psalm is as a teacher and ally of hope. With the steadiness of a metronome, this psalm repetitiously reasserts the trustworthiness of God's "firmly fixed" (v. 89) word/promise. And its 176 verse-after-verse-after-verse variations on the same theme serve to slow us readers down long enough to "get it," if we will. That is, to see that "the unfolding of your word gives light; it imparts understanding to the simple" (v. 130)—it engenders hope.

But this "unfolding" takes time. It does not happen casually or in a flash; but through protracted, attentive listening the gift appears. As the word becomes our "meditation all day long" (v. 97), we find hope. What I am calling imagination this psalm refers to as meditation (vv. 48, 148), or "treasuring" (v. 11), or "delighting in" (vv. 14, 16, 24, et. al.), or "fixing eyes upon" (v. 15). By whatever term, the point is that guidance from Elsewhere comes from studied attention being paid to a trustworthy source.

As Walker Percy writes: "To become aware of the possibility of the search is to be onto something. Not to be onto something is to be in despair"[4] This is the truth my friend Harold discovered as he worked alongside of homeless people for years. In the early years he was frequently irritated that so many of the homeless persons he befriended seemed to have little eagerness to better their lot. They were resigned to a life of pain and deprivation. But as Harold continued to listen, he discovered that a common denominator in their stories was the absence of any stable, dependable family or network. Chaos and broken promises were all they had known. Nothing in their lives had offered itself as solid enough to build upon. With this realization the scales fell from Harold's eyes.

Harold had been searching for evidences of hoping and striving, for the fruit of promise and imagination. But his friends did not have these source materials. Lacking any fixed promise-material, they had nothing to nurture any imagination of better stories for themselves. He came to understand that if he desired for his friends to live with hope, a key factor in that transformation was his own unquestionable dependability for them. He must become a living word that they might know hope.

It's often said that the best gift parents can give their children is the gift of roots and wings. We might translate those two as promise and imagination—and of the two, promise alone can be given. Parents can understand that job one for them is to nurture roots of good memories within their children, for without these roots it will be much harder for their children to find the wings of imagination to lift them to vistas of the possible. But with these in place, there is solid ground beneath their feet and worthy journeys beckoning them onward.

This rooting was evident in a thirty-ish mother who competed in an Alpha Male Ironman marathon. After completing the race in record time, she told her mother that mile after mile when her body and spirit seemed able to endure no more, her soul kept singing words she'd heard from childhood: "Glory be to the Father, and the to Son, and to the Holy Ghost. As it was in the beginning, is now, and ever shall be, world without end. Amen. Amen." Roots and wings.

The New Testament prayer introducing this meditation, a prayer that you "might know the hope to which [God] has called you" could be rephrased as a prayer for roots and wings. The roots mentioned are two stunning promises/ facts. The first is the hopefulness of seeing ourselves in a new way—not as objects of God's displeasure but as God's treasure, "a glorious inheritance." The second is the hopefulness of seeing God's power in a new way—not as indifferent or against us, but for us, "the immeasurable greatness of [God's] power for us." Neither of these is self-evident; they are, in fact, mind-blowing refutations of the often-felt. And because these are so different, the author knows it will take a special kind of comprehending to "get it."

And this brings us to the wings, to "the eyes of your heart" being opened to perceive the importance of these declarations. More than a quick first read is needed. Another word for this is imagination, the heart's ability to see beyond the apparent, the assumed, the limiting past and present. So, the essence of the prayer in Ephesians 1 is this: "May your word, O God, however and by whomever uttered, be met with inquisitive attention, with keen curiosity so that hope might be born and flourish." Or, to use the words of a hymn:

Open my eyes, that I may see
Glimpses of truth thou hast for me;
Place in my hands the wonderful key
That shall unclasp and set me free.[5]

NOTES

[1]"The Liberator," a Netflix miniseries, writer Jeb Stuart, adapted from Alex Kershaw, *The Liberator: One World War II Soldier's 500-Day Odyssey from the Beaches of Sicily to the Gates of Dachau* (New York: Crown, 2013).

[2]Felix L. Sparks, "Dachau and Its Liberation," June 15, 1989, http://www.45thinfantrydivision.com/index14.htm (accessed Dec. 2, 2020).

[3] Lynch, in *Images of Hope: Imagination as Healer of the Hopeless* (Notre Dame, IN: University of Notre Dame Press, 1974), deals with imagination as integral to hope. But he writes primarily from his work with the mentally ill whose sense of hopelessness is due to traumatized imaginations and who are in need of others' help in reviving damaged imagination. I wish to speak more generally of imagination as an essential component of hope in every circumstance and of its need for an objective basis in promise and promise-material. For imagination as a theological construct, see Garrett Green, "Imagination," in *A New Handbook of Christian Theology*, Donald Musser and Joseph Price, eds. (Nashville: Abingdon Press, 1992), 248-250; Garrett Green, *Imagining God: Theology and the Religious Imagination* (San Francisco: Harper & Row, 1989); Walter Brueggemann, *The Prophetic Imagination* (Philadelphia: Fortress Press, 1978). More pastoral treatments of imagination may be found in R.E.C. Browne, *The Ministry of the Word* (Philadelphia: Fortress Press, 1976) and Eugene Peterson, *Reversed Thunder: The Revelation of John and the Praying Imagination* (San Francisco: Harper & Row, 1988).

[4]Walker Percy, *The Moviegoer* (New York: Vintage, 1998), 13.

[5]Clara H. Scott, "Open My Eyes, That I May See," 1895.

The Man from Tomorrow

In the beginning was the Word, and the Word was with God, and the Word was God. He was in the beginning with God…. And the Word became flesh and lived among us, and we have seen his glory, the glory as of a father's only son, full of grace and truth.

(John 1:1-2, 14)

Enter most any Christian church around the world, be it grand or plain, and the symbol most likely to greet your eye will be a cross or crucifix. But this was not always the case. The cross was never depicted in the art of the Church's first centuries. The wall paintings of the earliest churches and catacombs were of Jesus the Good Shepherd, of Jesus walking on water, of Jesus healing the paralytic—not a cross, not Jesus on a cross. He is always shown as the active, living Savior. When the iconography of the Eastern church began to show the scene centuries later, it never depicted him as a slumping figure on an instrument of death but as "a live Christ on the Cross—head up with open eyes—the Christ who triumphs over death even at the moment of crucifixion."[1]

This is not to say Jesus' crucifixion was ignored by the early churches—the sermons, the letters, the records of their lives show their reverence for Jesus' death. But when it came to their worship and their spiritual fascination, it was the resurrection that thrilled them. What had happened at Golgotha was, of course, of immense importance, but what had happened at the garden tomb was the astonishing exclamation point. The Resurrection was the crowning good news, a victory over the fatalism, futility, and death that gripped their world. Jesus had brought vitality and joy to them and within days of his death and resurrection, they were displaying "glad and generous hearts, praising God" and speaking of him and acting in his name with "boldness."

The Cross and the Resurrection were a culmination of a story that stretches all the way back to God's Abraham promises and reaches all the way out to the infinity of God's forever. Its dramatic turning point came, not at Golgotha, but on Easter morning when God finally tilted the story upward toward the "all is well" finale of all things. The Resurrection freed every stick, stone, and star; every tree and sea; every four-legged beast and two-legged human; every planet, platypus, and polecat—yes, the whole universe—to join the ultimate "hallelujah chorus." In New Testament thought, Jesus is far more than a bloodied victim stuck on a stick in ancient history. His death/

resurrection is the key that opens humanity's prison door and releases earth's story to its blessed intention. He is the "Man from Tomorrow" who calls us to follow him in joyful hope to the glad consummation of the cosmos.

By introducing this self-made term "Man from Tomorrow," I am reaching back to an idea I introduced in the Curious Cat meditation. There I spoke of the God who is out ahead of us, coming to us from the future and calling us into God's future. I said that just as life and death come to us from the future, so does God. An early biblical indication of this comes when God spoke to Moses from a burning bush (Exodus 3), revealing God's holy, covenant name, YHWH. Though we've learned to translate YHWH as meaning "I am that I am," many interpreters think it is better translated as "he who proves himself"[2]—that is, the God who will act and speak in trustworthy ways in days to come. Or, as German philosopher Ernst Bloch put it, our God has "future as his essential nature."[3] More plainly said, God's habitat is Tomorrow.

Jesus comes to us from God, as emissary from that habitat, from "a land that is fairer than day." Yes, if you wish to get even more traditional, he comes from the "sweet by and by" we commonly call heaven. It's what is out in front of us, prepared, ready, waiting. But from that Tomorrow, from God's future, Jesus comes into a broken, yearning world that is casting about for relief, for healing, for hope.

Most importantly, Jesus didn't tell a groaning world to hunker down and wait stoically for that tomorrow. Rather, he spoke of his Father's habitat becoming an operative power today. He taught us to pray for God's kingdom to come; that is, for God's tomorrow to enter our wondrous/waste land now. And as an ambassador from God's Tomorrow, Jesus performed deeds that demonstrated God's future released in our now. He shared food, welcomed outcasts, checked sickness, defanged nature, forgave sins, shamed bullies, and caused hope to blossom. "Blessed are the eyes that see what you see," he said, "For I tell you many prophets and kings desired to see what you see, but did not see it, and to hear what you hear, but did not hear it" (Luke 10:23). The world, under Jesus' touch, looked like God's tomorrow today.

If we are to hear this message rightly, we must read it remembering God's Abrahamic promise to bless all the families of the earth through Abraham. This connection between Jesus and this ancient promise begins to come into focus when Moses leads Abraham's descendants out of their bondage as slaves in Egypt to land that Abraham and Sarah had lived in centuries before. This exodus is the model instance when YHWH "proves himself" as a compassionate, promise-keeping God who opens doors and leads hope-starved people into better tomorrows. Arriving on the Abrahamic strip of "promise" land, they form a tiny nation amid formidable world powers and become a buffer between giants and often a pawn or staging area for their wars. The Old Testament narrates their perilous existence, their brief span of glorious regional dominance when David (and then Solomon) was their king, and then their tailspin into national division and the countless, profitless survival bargains made with their "big boy" neighbors.

Finally, their nationalist dreams all come to naught. The descendants of Abraham and Sarah lose it all—land, nation, freedom. The only thing still in their possession is the ancient promise and the hope that YHWH will again bless them and make Abraham's people great. Israel's prophets, fired by the promise, preached and wrote about this good time coming in words that soar with defiance and hope:

> The word of the LORD [will go forth] from Jerusalem. He shall judge between the nations, and shall arbitrate for many peoples; they shall beat their swords into plowshares, and their spears into pruning hooks; nation shall not lift up sword against nation, neither shall they learn war any more. (Isa. 2:3-4)

> Then the eyes of the blind shall be opened, and the ears of the deaf unstopped; then the lame shall leap like a deer, and the tongue of the speechless sing for joy. (Isa. 35:5-6)

> For surely I know the plans I have for you, says the LORD, plans for your welfare and not for harm, to give you a future with hope. (Jer. 29:11)

It was into this context and yearning, simmering for centuries, that Jesus came and taught, and after three years of tomorrow deeds and teaching he came to Jerusalem in its highest holy season. There he was greeted by glad shouts: "Hosanna! Blessed is the one who comes in the name of the LORD! Blessed is the coming kingdom of our ancestor David! Hosanna in the highest heaven!" The people welcomed him as the messiah, the champion who would drive out the occupying Romans and usher in the day of their prophets' visions. But the Romans viewed it differently. They understandably saw him as a threat to their rule and within the week they nailed this preacher to a cross, a felon guilty of insurrection.

But it is the Christian insistence that this was not the end of the story. As in all the days before, God was at work carving good even from this sordid deed of history. Jesus' followers insisted that on the following Sunday, they saw him alive—he spoke with them, they ate with him. He promised he would never forsake them but would be with them always, even to the end of the age.

Some of them, however, went far beyond saying, "He lives!" They said that in Jesus the incredible had happened. Not only had ancient promises been honored, an event of cosmic significance had occurred! They said the "Man from Tomorrow" had given this earth new birth. According to them, when Jesus died, the whole writhing creation was carried by him into the tomb. In Jesus' death, creation was put to death. And when God raised Jesus from death, the whole creation was also raised up. The stranglehold of the past had been broken. In Jesus, they claimed, there is a new creation! Upon this blood-soaked land of grief and pain God's tomorrow had come! "The darkness is passing away and the true light is already shining" (1 John 2:8).

Dawn! To be sure, tomorrow's coming was not fully here; the fullness of it still lay in the future. But something world-changing had happened: the tomb of our death had been shattered and God's Tomorrow was now rushing in like a rising tide! And this wasn't going to be like a new Roman Empire or a revived kingdom of Israel; it was uniquely God's tomorrow recreating the here and now in beauty, justice, and neighborliness. God's "kingdom" had come near and was now to be entered.

This, in fact, is what Jesus himself announced at the beginning of his ministry: "Jesus came proclaiming the good news of God, and saying, 'The time is fulfilled, and the kingdom of God has come near, repent, and believe in the good news'" (Mark 1:14-15). From day one, Jesus' good news had been that the longed-for tomorrow was near and his invitation was to believe in its presence. The world as it is was being "invaded" by the world of God's intent, and all were welcome to enter the wonder and the challenge of it—now!

My suspicion is that for many people in America today—even those who attend church—Jesus is just the poor sucker who got strung up by the Romans, the classic proof that nice guys can't survive in this jungle. To others, Jesus is mostly the heaven-securing One who died to pay for their sins—a saintly hero to be thanked but not necessarily followed. For both groups, Jesus' death ranks more prominently than his resurrection. In direct contrast with our texts and earliest history, the crucifixion rather than the resurrection holds the most fascination. And because this is so, the cosmic hope that throbs through the New Testament has become a modest trickle today. Easter now is a spring break holiday—not the day that broke the devil's back. The Jesus of a "new world now" has been dumped into the church's archives as an idealistic curiosity piece.

But Jesus is not a religious relic! He is as much alive as you are—even more so—and livelier than anyone whose flesh you can touch. On more than one occasion his spirit-presence has put steel into my timid spine and wrapped gentle arms around these sad shoulders. I've seen him get hold of messed-up folks and turn them into more admirable humans than even a praying momma ever dared to dream. In short, I've seen him "fix" folks. But more than that, I've often felt and feel him out front of us, begging *us* to "fix" some other things—hunger, racism, loneliness, our own hypocrisy. As much as he is with us, he so often appears as distant as an impatient pioneer on a far horizon waving to us to come on and catch up.

Thank God, after all these years, he still remains with us, this Man from Tomorrow,

…whose death put to death our bondage to the past,
…whose resurrection certifies who's now in charge,
…whose gift is a new creation loosed in this groaning one,
…whose life converts scaredy-cats into brave souls,
…whose spirit creates communities of tomorrow-people, and
…whose promise to complete God's dream gives lively hope.

This Jesus implants the crazy notion that we can be and do more than our crimped little imaginations conceive—that we can be more like Jesus than Adam and live in a world more like Eden than Babylon. And on our journey to those destinations, we may dare believe that even when the worst thing possible happens, so will an impossible mercy; and when we can't go on, grace will lift us up; and when death for the moment wins, God will not be defeated.

NOTES

[1]Marchita Mauck, "Visual Arts," in *The Oxford History of Christian Worship*, Geoffrey Wainwright and Karen Westerfield Tucker, eds. (New York: Oxford University Press, 2006), 818-820.

[2]Hans Walter Wolff, *Anthropology of the Old Testament* (SCM Press, 2012), 152. Wolff is among many who understand the name to have a future force.

[3]Cited by Jürgen Moltmann, *Theology of Hope* (Fortress Press, 1993), 16.

PART 2
Living in Lively Hope

Through [Christ] you have come to trust in God,
who raised him from the dead and gave him glory,
so that your faith and hope are set on God.
(1 Pet. 1:21 NIV)

Hope appears
when the mud beneath us
licks our toes.

We can't own it.
Eventually the sun claims it,
drinks its moisture
making it
something different,
something the wind covets.

But it is real, isn't it?
When it crawls
between our toes
on rainy Sundays.

It isn't always reliable
like clocks, for instance,
or rain gauges.

Still, it isn't unreliable,
never sullen
with the noon heat or angry
when the wind rages.

Maybe it lives its own life
somewhere in the reaches of blue,
and breathes with us
when we remember
the sky tangles with mud
as easily as it stretches to
another universe.

—Carol Bell

"Where Hope Lives" (for Czeslaw Milosz), *The Geography of Hope: Poets of Colorado's Western Slope*, David Rothman, ed. (Crested Butte, CO: Conundrum Press, 1998), 9.

Serving a Slow God[1]

*And Abram said, "You have given me no offspring, and so a slave born in
my house is to be my heir." But the word of the LORD came to him, "This
man shall not be your heir." He brought him outside and said, "Look toward
heaven and count the stars, if you are able to count them." Then he said to
him, "So shall your descendants be."*

(Gen. 15:3-6)

Speed does not seem to be one of God's strong suits—at least according to
the Abram story. That unwelcome fact is for me a prominent takeaway from
the man's story.

Abram is already seventy-five years old when we first see his name, tucked
into a genealogy of descendants of Noah's son Shem. The only notable fact
given about him is that he and his wife Sarai have "no child." When I ran the
numbers on Abram's male forebears (using the data in the Genesis 11 genealogy), I discovered that on average they'd all fathered children before they were
forty-four. So, having "no child" at age seventy-five is attention-getting. But
what is not attention-getting is Abram's piety. Not one word is said about
his religious fervor. If he has a starring role in this show, it wasn't awarded by
virtue of his virtue.

The truth is, Abram is just a childless, aging, ordinary guy. He is what
the Germans call a *jedermann*, an everyone, an anyone. He is the thin-haired
retiree walking out of Walmart, wearing scuffed sneakers, hitched-too-high
Dockers, and a faded flannel shirt—a rumpled, wrinkled grandpa type,
except that this grandpa has no grandkids, not even any kids. But what this
jedermann does have is the experience of hearing YHWH utter a promise
of land, descendants, and blessing. And what this *jedermann* has is the
experience of spending all his remaining Tuesdays—a century's worth of
them—traipsing around in tents, betting everything on the trustworthiness
of this promise-making God.

It was no Sunday School picnic. There was, for starters, the near-disaster
of a trek down to Egypt when he tried to pass off his still-gorgeous wife as his
sister in an attempt to avoid being killed himself. (I'm still shaking my head
over that one. What *was* the old guy thinking?) Then there was a parting of
ways with his tagalong nephew Lot because their joint flocks grew too large
for any one region to sustain them. But that parting then caused Abram to
be dragged into a war, becoming a reluctant warrior fighting to rescue this

nephew who wasn't worth saving in the first place. So his life went, year after year, with YHWH and his promises fading into deeper questionability.

Finally, well into this odyssey, Abram brings up the sensitive subject once again, complaining to YHWH that he is still childless, not to mention still "on the road" even in Canaan. For his complaint he receives an impressive planetarium show (see above) and a smokin' menagerie-like psychedelic "vision" (see Genesis 15), assuring him the promises were still valid.

Nonetheless, another decade passes without a baby's cry being heard in Abram's tent or a deed of land entering his hands. Overwhelmed by disappointment and ditching all the niceties of marriage, he takes the initiative and fathers an heir (Ishmael) with his wife's handmaid. Still, YHWH remains mute, saying nothing at all—not even about Ishmael—until the boy is a teenager. Then, when God finally shows up again, disqualifying Abram's "Ishmael initiative" and repeating the old promise of a child, Abram laughs in God's face—as does Sarai when she later hears the same. God responds by changing their names to Abraham and Sarah. As though a change of names was going to alter their childless, landless estate.

All told, twenty-five long years pass between the speaking of the promise and the report that finally says:

> The LORD dealt with Sarah as he had said, and the LORD did for Sarah as he had promised. Sarah conceived and bore Abraham a son in his old age… Abraham gave the name Isaac to his son whom Sarah bore him…. Abraham was a hundred years old when his son Isaac was born to him. Now Sarah said, "God has brought laughter for me, everyone who hears will laugh with me." And she said, "Who would ever have said to Abraham that Sarah would nurse children? Yet I have borne him a son in his old age." (Gen. 21:1-7)

My imagination freezes when I try to picture the sight and sound of a ninety-year-old "Madonna and child." The scene is no more imaginable today than it was three millennia ago. Fittingly, they named the child Isaac, the Hebrew word for laughter. It's a good name and frame for this family portrait. For here is the deep, wondrous laughter of the faithfulness of God verified—the laughter of hope fulfilled. An "I can't believe the softness of this little guy's skin upon my leathered-old fingers" laughter.

But it was so very overdue! Sarah had prayed and waited for a child all her adult years. And for the last twenty-five of them she'd been dangling on a promise from God. To compound the anguish of it all, she would enjoy laughter with Isaac for only thirty-seven years before she died. And when she died, poor old Abraham had to buy a burial plot from a Canaanite—he didn't yet own even a 3-foot x 6-foot plot of dirt, let alone have "a land" to call his own!

In this book's introduction I used Carlo Caretto's "speeding astronaut in a pierced space capsule" metaphor for our age. In contrast, so much of what the Bible offers us seems so laughably slow and out of date. We cry out for a "fast" God or One who can at least keep pace with a Wells Fargo stagecoach! But Mary and Joseph's pokey donkey, as comical as the tortoise and the hare, testifies to a God whose sure mercies aren't always delivered with the click of your cursor. Something more amazing than quick fixes is this God's pace. And those who wish to join this God will have to reckon on some herculean adjustments of time and life ambitions.

I've sometimes wondered how Abraham later assessed his life. After Sarah's death, in the hush of nightfall when evening fires hypnotize their watchers and spit occasional embers toward faraway, silent stars—in those quiet hours when old men review the journey of their life—what was Abraham's verdict on his life? Did he die with a hallelujah on his lips, a smile of gratitude softening his eyes? Or did he die wondering what all his years had really accomplished? Had he played the fool, wasting his life as a pathetic victim of religious fanaticism? Might Sarah have borne him a son sooner had she not been subjected to his wandering schemes and dreams? Hope can be a cruel master. Had it made a joke of him?

There's no way for us to know Abraham's thoughts. That answer is hidden from us, just as the significance of our own lives is hidden from us. We muddle through its daily installments, busy with whatever is on our plate and sometimes we off-ramp long enough to ask the meaning questions only to arrive at unsatisfactory, provisional maybes. We hope we're playing it right! But it's tough to tell. The slowness of God to shine a reassuring light on our path often puzzles, and the scoreboard is never reliably visible either. How can any mortal satisfactorily measure the meaning of her days? She can't!

But if the significance of our own life is unknowable, we can measure the significance of Abraham's—and from his story harvest some hope for our own. We'd have to begin with the astonishing fact that we're still talking about Abraham—and his life! Though he could never have dreamt it, Abraham's improbable sojourn still sets the standard, thousands of years later, for the majority of the world for what faith looks like. Judaism, Christianity, and Islam all look to Father Abraham as the fountainhead of their faith. He is known by name on every continent, and his biological and spiritual descendants cover the face of the earth as surely as a blanket of stars covers it every night. "All the families of the earth," including Abraham's, have been variously blessed through this one man's life.

Who then can know how many or how far the ripples may flow from one splashing pebble? Or, who can say how many centuries God's resolve to fully bless "all the families of the earth" will need for its fulfillment, or the paths it may take to reach its promised destinations? God seems in no hurry to tell us the "big stuff"—no more than God seems to interrupt our breakfasts to inform us of the score and time remaining in our little life. So, it seems that the task before us is to look to Father Abraham with student eyes, noting his every move, and to trust the best promises we ourselves have heard. Like Abraham and Sarah, we walk by faith and not by sight. We trust where we cannot see. We hope.

And yes, this means we may often feel like one of those tiny dots pointillist painters daub on their canvas. The value of our presence is easy to discount, being just one pinpoint of ink smushed up against and among a zillion other tiny, seemingly insignificant dots. Unfortunately, the dark jungle of our placement doesn't allow us to see any big picture being crafted. But because of Abraham, we have reason to hope that maybe we are playing our good part in the grand mural being painted ever so slowly by Earth's most trustworthy artist, the God of Abraham and Sarah and Isaac.

NOTES

[1] I am indebted to Richard Mouw for the title, "Serving a Slow God." It appears as a chapter title in his *Uncommon Decency: Christian Civility in an Uncivil World* (Downers Grove, IL: Intervarsity Press, 1992).

Life in Two Time Zones

God has rescued us from the power of darkness
and transferred us into the kingdom of his beloved Son,
in whom we have redemption, the forgiveness of sins.
(Col. 1:13-14)

Kendall, Kansas is in the far western part of that state, on US Highway 50, just twenty-five miles or so from the Colorado state line. I guess I have driven through it at least a dozen times. I confess, however, that I don't remember the place. It's what motorists call "a wide spot in the road"—although I am sure the folks in Kendall feel differently. Even so, according to my maps, Kendall, Kansas does have one very notable distinction. The line separating the Central Time Zone from the Mountain Time Zone runs right through Kendall.

Google says Kendall officially runs on Mountain Time, but I can't help wondering how often folks out there have to double check when they're due someplace. "Is that my time, or yours?" sounds like a question you might hear with some frequency—especially if you're doing business in Lakin, fifteen miles to the east (Central Time), or in Syracuse, twelve miles west (Mountain Time).

Determining what time zone you are operating in is a constant assignment for hopers, too. That's because of the way God messed up all our clocks and charts through the resurrection of Jesus.

The people of Jesus' day seem to have had a pretty clear idea of when the resurrection was to happen: "someday." And the "someday" they had in mind was the "last day," the day when the trumpet would sound and the promised good time coming, the reign of God on earth, would ensue. This is certainly the way Mary of Bethany understood it when she told Jesus, "I know that [my dead brother, Lazarus] will rise again in the resurrection on the last day" (John 11:24).

But Mary never imagined that resurrection was nearer than she thought—today! The possibility did not enter her mind that the promised good time coming was at hand—now! Indeed, no one seems to have seen this coming. That God—the "slow God" of Abraham—might actually jumpstart the last days with an invasion today of tomorrow's life: this was a mind-bender! But this is precisely what happened, in the middle of history rather than at "the last day," Jesus was raised from the dead by the power of God.

The upshot was that Jesus' followers realized they were now living in two time zones: this present age and the age to come. On one hand, through their association with Jesus they had "tasted the powers of the age to come" (Heb. 6:5). The promised kingdom of God—which they had calendared for "someday"—was now already "in their midst" (Luke 17:21). They had been "rescued from the power of darkness and transferred into the kingdom of God's beloved Son." But on the other hand, they still were "in" this world, even if no longer wholly "of" it (see John 15:19, et al). Jesus' resurrection had relocated them from being residents to being "pilgrims," "aliens," and "strangers" in their own land. They now were holders of dual citizenship, demonstrably born of flesh and blood but also born of the Spirit, and thus attuned to a future frequency—participants in an impinging glorious future that was already filtering into this world and certain to transform it from top to bottom.

And so we still are, people who are called to live today as though God's promised tomorrow was already here. And, indeed, it *is* already here—in part. There's ever so much more to come when the LORD returns, but for the time being we are to live as early indicators of a future that cannot be denied.

Consider this analogy: One might say that every tomorrow begins at midnight, with the passing from p.m. to a.m. Even so, for five or six hours, tomorrow—though already truly present—remains shrouded. Only with the faint hints of dawn does tomorrow register on waiting eyes. Just so, God's tomorrow began in the darkness of Golgotha—and though we still wait for its full noonday, . For the moment we may be as one who "walks in darkness and has no light, yet trusts in the name of the LORD and relies upon his God" (Isa. 50:10). But the dawn and its subsequent bright noonday cannot be cancelled. They are certain. This is but an analogy, but I offer it as one way to comprehend our place and task. We live in today's world under divine orders to exemplify tomorrow's world.

Joe Yelder's story may be our own. Joe was a tall, soft-spoken man, a deacon in the First Baptist Church of Selma, Alabama, the oldest Black church in that city. He also was an admired public school administrator, having earned an enviable reputation across fifteen years in the 1960s and 1970s as the principal of Hudson High School, Selma's Black high school. But when the courts finally mandated that the city's schools must integrate, Joe Yelder became the reluctant center of political contention in Selma.

He was passed over as the principal of the city's new, racially integrated high school; that job was given to a white man, and Yelder agreed to be the principal of one of the newly formed junior high schools. Many members in the Black community, however, were irate, convinced by long experience that Yelder's lesser assignment was race-based. They urged him to sue the school board for the slight. Yelder protested: "I'm an educator, not a civil rights fighter."

According to J.L. Chestnut Jr., a friend and local attorney, Joe "was geared by nature and experience to the old era of accommodation." He "was a product of his generation—born in 1910, not that far from slavery. It ran against his grain to buck anybody, especially white authority." But when the tomorrow of integration came, Yelder "happened to be the one person in a position to stand up for black people because he had the most seniority."

Yelder eventually yielded to the pressure coming from Chestnut and the Black community. He sued the school board and won; he was hired as principal of the new Selma High School and awarded back pay. But after a year in the position, he resigned, telling Chestnut: "I've paid my dues…. You were right, and that's why I did it. But I've earned the right not to live under all this strain."[1]

Yelder's story appears in Chestnut's autobiography in a chapter he titled: "Straddling Two Eras." That is how Chestnut saw his friend's plight. And that is how we might profitably see our own position. Like Yelder, neither by nature nor by experience are we geared to see ourselves as agents of a coming era. (My own comfort zone nestles next to the villages of Fit In and Go Along.) Hence, we are likely to be no more disposed than Yelder to confront the existing order or to model a threatening alternative. We ask, who am I to be the one who walks the plank? The Braveheart who protests injustice? Yet, this is the assignment of those who are privileged to live in the overlapping of the ages. We are the ones to *do* the Sermon on the Mount, the ones to live on less in order that others may simply live, the ones to champion the cause of those whom others find unacceptable, the ones whose valuing is out of sync with the way things are. Indeed, we are "a peculiar people" (1 Pet. 2:9 KJV) whose hope has put us in a different time zone.

But within our "peculiarness" there is also a deep joy, for we are lighting a path of hope. Is not the global landscape covered with "No Exit" signs warning us of the unsustainability of our present addiction to profits, pleasure, and power? Can we not hear the rage of denied dignity coming from those whose skin color or ethnicity is not dominant? Can we not see the handwriting on the wall? So, the privilege of modeling God's tomorrow as a sign of hope within a staggering world—there is deep joy in this assignment. It is the joy of living in and leading others into God's better world.

I relish the taste of tomorrow that has been served up every Thursday night for a quarter of a century by a church I know. Beginning around four o'clock in the afternoon a homeless crowd begins to assemble outside its building, a crowd unfortunately still not likely to be seen inside on Sunday mornings. But in an hour or so, Sunday-morning people will sit down with Thursday-night guests and share with them a generous and gratis white tablecloth meal of warm food, conversation included. These two crowds, whose worlds and stories are planets apart, yet share in almost out-of-body moments at those tables; something much grander than "charity" is felt. I think the word for it is thoughtfulness, or perhaps dignity? Maybe the word is hope. Whatever it is, at least for an hour or so it feels somewhat like what I think tomorrow will be, except that it's been going on for twenty-five years now in the fellowship hall of a Baptist church "deep in the heart of Texas."

I read about a woman who all by herself managed to feed, clothe, and educate eight children in a bayou tar-paper shack. When an interviewer asked how she'd done it, she said: "I seen a new world coming." Some folks I know, though not at all "rich" by American standards, nonetheless receive thousands of dollars each year on retirement investments, a portion of which Uncle Sam dictates must be annually withdrawn and put back into circulation. So, their needs being disciplined and minimal, they choose—in addition to their tithes—to give those required withdrawals to agencies and groups who, like that bayou lady, have also "seen a new world coming." Another believer I know, skilled in listening, finds thoughtful ways to speak of Jesus, the man from tomorrow, to despairing folks. Every now and then one of his listeners chooses to become a participant in that world, and follows Jesus. There is a way for every two-time-zone child of God to show up, speak up, and ante up as a harbinger of God's new world coming.

In the years I served as a church pastor I dreaded those Sundays when the nation's clocks changed from and to Daylight Savings Time. Even the clever slogans of "spring forward" and "fall back" began to sound like death knells. Regardless of how many reminders we gave to our members, when those dreaded Sundays arrived, there were always those who would arrive during the benediction or who told us later that they came early and, realizing they'd have to wait, went to IHOP and let the time get away from them. If I'd ever thought I knew which D.C. bureaucrat was really in charge of that semi-annual farce, I would have told them a thing or two…beginning with the question of why they chose Sundays as the day to activate this freakish upset. No doubt about it, I would have let 'em have it with both barrels—in Christian love, of course!

But if I were still in pastoral harness, I now think I might almost be grateful for those semi-annual time resets. If nothing more, they remind churchgoers that we are people for whom the times are always out of joint. We are tomorrow people living today as witnesses to a future that, though unseen, is more certain than sunrise. In fact, I might even come to see that a primary gift of assembling each week is to help us recalibrate our clocks *every* Sunday, assessing where we spent last week and determining where we want to dwell this coming one. For us, the far-off is already inexplicably near, and the someday reign of God is now knocking at the world's door.

NOTE

[1]J.L. Chestnut Jr. and Julia Cass, *Black in Selma: The Uncommon Life of J.L. Chestnut Jr.* (New York: Farrar, Straus and Giroux, 1990), 284-295.

The Grandest Gamble

God is our refuge and strength, a very present help in trouble. Therefore we will not fear, though the earth should change, though the mountains shake in the heart of the sea; though its waters roar and foam, though the mountains tumble with its tumult… "Be still and know that I am God! I am exalted among the nations; I am exalted in the earth." The LORD *of hosts is with us; the God of Jacob is our refuge.*

(Ps. 46:1-3, 16-17)

You won't find arguments for the existence of God in the Bible. God is the Bible's foundational assumption. Atheism isn't its problem; idolatry is. Believing in non-gods is the problem. One biblical writer, exemplifying the conviction of all, throws up his hands at one point, exasperatedly saying: "You believe in God? Well, whoopedoo! Even the *demons* believe in God!" (my very free translation of Jas. 2:19, italics added.)

Believing can be little more than a talisman, a warm fuzzy in a cold world. Believing costs nothing. Oh, it might cost a moment's embarrassment when the subject of God comes up in the corner booth at IHOP and you sheepishly admit to your companions that you're a believer, hoping they won't lump you with devotees of the Great Pumpkin—but in our society there's usually no penalty for being a believer. But if you *bet* on God, the stakes are very different.

If you bet on God, it does cost you something—if not in the favor of your friends, then in your manner of life. For when you bet—on anything —you put some skin in the game. You invest, you stretch, you stick your neck out, you risk. The grandest gamble you can ever make is to bet on God.

Hope might be defined as a skin-in gamble on the fidelity and ability of God. It is behavior that says you not only believe there is a God, but that this God is also present, working for the good, the beautiful, and the true; and this God has a lively, vested interest in those who hang on, dig in, and pony up—especially when the odds are long. Even when the cards say the game is over, hope doubles down on the promises of God. Those who hope are in effect tipping their hand, revealing that they are playing the long game. They live on less, give more, back the unlikely, attempt the improbable, and sometimes feel uncomfortably "out of it."

Just as love is belief expressed in space, hope is belief extended in time.[1] Hope converts belief into an expensive, delicious adventure; it puts belief on the road. That's why it is the grandest gamble—not just the greatest one—because if you're correct, the payoff more than matches the anticipated, and the journey to get there is often hair-raisingly fascinating.

But if God doesn't come through, you stand to lose more than you dare tally.

So, the most searching question we can ask ourselves is this: Is God indeed trustworthy? Dare you bet your one and, so far as we know, only life on the notion that "behind the dim unknown standeth God within the shadow, keeping watch above his own"?[2] A promise is worth no more than the promiser. So, what can we say about the trustworthiness of God?

One might expect nothing but five-star reviews coming from the Bible on this question, but that is not so. For instance, the prophet Jeremiah wonders if God hasn't been to him like "a deceitful brook" (15:20)—like waters that fail—and accuses God of being a con artist (20:7) who has duped him into preaching ideas so outrageous that he's become little more than a late-night TV joke.

Another accuser says God "has driven and brought me into darkness without any light" and declares God "is a bear lying in wait for me, a lion in hiding; he led me off my way and tore me to pieces." In consequence he has "forgotten what happiness is" and can only say, "Gone is my glory, and all that I had hoped for from the LORD" (Lam. 3:2, 10-11, 17-18).

And then there is Job, valued by God as "a blameless and upright man" like "no one [else] on earth" (Job 1:8). Yet he is shockingly turned over to relentless, satanic sieges in a bizarre kind of test. And from the ash heap of his life, Job moans: "Oh, that I knew where I might find [God], that I might come even to [God's] dwelling! I would lay my case before [God]" and secure justice. But the Holy One seems to have an unlisted number and whoever's in charge at headquarters has departed the planetary premises without the courtesy of a forwarding address (23:3-4, 8-9). Too, more than one psalmist comes to the witness stand, virtually accusing God of indifference:

> How long, O LORD, will you look on?
> > Do not let my treacherous enemies rejoice over me!
> You have seen, O LORD, do not be silent!
> > O LORD, do not be far from me! Wake up!
> Bestir yourself for my defense, for my cause,
> > my God and my LORD." (Ps. 35:17, 19, 22-23)

And though I'd like to ignore it, there is the point-blank question/accusation quoted by the Gambler from Nazareth from a Roman cross: "My God, my God, why have you forsaken me?" (Ps. 22:1).

And what shall we say of the millions since Bible days who certainly seem to have heartbreaking grounds to sue God for misrepresentation? Even if these be minority reports, this is stout evidence that even within the Bible God is not a sure bet—at least not in the ways we typically use the word "sure."

Questions about the character and the power of the Promiser rest at the heart of all our hopes. And in their raw, insistent complexity they will push their way again and again into these pages, spitting in the face of sugary chirps of "happily ever after."

So, one way to begin the crucial conversation may be with William Sloane Coffin's observation that "if we misconceive God as Father Protector, as one, so to speak, in charge of all the uncontrolled contingencies along the way, then each disappointment reduces what may confidently be affirmed about God. And this is how people lose their faith." Coffin insists we must begin to think of God as providing "minimum protection-maximum support— support to help us grow up, to stretch our minds and hearts until they are as wide as God's universe." For him, this means we will "stop blaming God for being absent when we ourselves were not present, stop blaming God for the ills of the world as if we had been laboring to cure them, and stop making God responsible for all the thinking and doing we should be undertaking on our own."[3] Coffin is ladling out brimming doses of strong medicine in these words, and, even if he is speaking truth, his words may wisely be paired with C.S. Lewis' softer, rescuing discovery.

Lewis, a professor of English literature at Oxford University, came to Christian faith well into adulthood and to marriage well after that. Only in his fifties did this confirmed bachelor meet, fall in love with, and marry an American divorcee, Joy Davidman. She was suffering from cancer when they married, but miraculously, she soon recovered, and for three years the two of them enjoyed an idyllic marriage. But then the cancer returned and within weeks it took her life. Lewis was devastated.

He had always kept a diary, and even in the dark days of Joy's dying, Lewis continued to do so. Decades later he was persuaded to publish this portion of his diary as a book, *A Grief Observed*. Using the accumulated word power of a lifelong lover of language, Lewis had spilled onto these pages his unedited rage and grief, the fury of one who felt monstrously cheated by

God. No psalmist, no Jeremiah or Job screams any louder than Lewis in his accusations of divine betrayal. But as Lewis continues to walk through this lonely dark tunnel, the reader notices that he begins to evaluate his experience differently.

He begins to reconsider the fairness of his own expectations of God, to wonder if he had consistently misinterpreted the promises of God. With this reappraisal of his crucible, Lewis comes to realize that God had been present in ways that grief had blocked from his vision, in saving ways that did honor the ancient promises. To be sure, they were honored in ways he had not foreseen or understood at the time, but they were honored. As a consequence, Lewis became a more careful, quiet student of God's ways. He still had his questions; he still ached with grief. But the trustworthy Companion was still with him.

Throughout our life—and certainly within these pages—questions about the trustworthiness and goodness of God will and must arise. To ignore them is unhelpful; to face them is a first step toward finding credible hope. My hunch, however, is that though pilgrims from Jeremiah and Job to Bill Coffin and C.S. Lewis have left notes for our guidance, when faith's affirmations become our soul's sad quest, each of us must find our own "aha!" moment and overhear for ourselves the word that illumines a path.

In one hour of my own deep need, that word came through hearing an unfortunately, often-omitted stanza of Georg Neumark's haunting hymn, "If You Will Trust in God to Guide You."

> What gain is there in futile weeping,
> In helpless anger and distress?
> If you are in God's care and keeping,
> In sorrow will God love you less?
> For he who took for you a cross
> Will bring you safe through ev'ry loss.[4]

The story goes that Georg Neumark (1621–1681), when only twenty years of age, was mugged by bandits as he traveled to study law at the University of Konigsberg. The thieves left him with nothing but his prayer book and a small sum of money he had sewn into the hem of the coat he was wearing. Bloodied and nearly destitute, he limped his way to a nearby town, sought the aid of a pastor, and waited long months before finally gaining employment as a tutor for a wealthy family's children. Only after two years was he able to resume his journey and his studies and eventually become a respected man of letters. But from the devastation of this experience Neumark distilled this poetic testimony. It is a testimony whose power I have always felt is enhanced by being expressed mostly in gentle questions and reminders rather than in loud pronouncements. Such is the quiet, tender need of all who, wounded by life, seek assurance that "God will help...when the morning dawns" (Ps. 46:5b).

At the risk of seeming to conclude this meditation with a splash of cheap devotional cologne, I must, in fairness, report that the "bear" and "lion" accuser mentioned earlier (Lamentations 3), goes on to add these lines in verses 19-25:

The thought of my affliction and my homelessness
    is wormwood and gall!
My soul continually thinks of it
    and is bowed down within me.
But this I call to mind,
    and therefore I have hope:

The steadfast love of the LORD never ceases,
    his mercies never come to an end;
they are new every morning;
    great is your faithfulness.
"The LORD is my portion," says my soul,
    "therefore I will hope in him."

The LORD is good to those who wait for him,
    to the soul that seeks him.

I wish we had been given some clues as to how this came to be the writer's testimony. But lacking that, I must take note that here is a gambler who is finding the journey and its God to be excruciatingly grand. Hope lives.

NOTES

[1]The relationship of the three theological virtues of faith, hope, and love is fascinating. I like the way Collin Morris expressed it: "These are not random virtues practiced by the Christian; they are the essential dimensions of the Christian life, which is defective if it neglects any of the three. *Hope* is possible because the one who follows the way of Christ has *faith* that there is no human situation, however unpromising, which is impervious to *love*. Here are the three pillars on

which the Kingdom of God is raised in the life of the individual believer—faith venturing beyond the unprovable, love forgiving the unpardonable, and hope remaining undimmed against all odds. And the character of personal discipleship is mirrored in the Christian community—Faith defines the Church, Love holds it together, Hope keeps it in existence. And these qualities do not float like a vapor in thin air. They are called forth by encounter with the Risen Christ. It is faith *in* him, love *for* him, and hope *from* him which make for the wholeness of Christian experience." *Bugles in the Afternoon* (Philadelphia: Westminster Press, 1977), 24-25.

[2]James Russell Lowell, "The Present Crisis."

[3]William Sloane Coffin, *Credo* (Louisville, KY: Westminster John Knox Press, 2004), 16,10.

[4]Stanza copyright owned by Augsburg Publishing House; reprinted by permission of Augsburg Fortress.

Wasting Time or Waiting Well?

The Lord *is good to those who wait for him, to the soul that seeks him.*
It is good that one should wait quietly for the salvation of the Lord.
(Lam. 3:25-26)

Not that you need this information, but I have only three speeding tickets on my record—and one of those was issued by a policeman who clearly was trying to meet some quota for the number of tickets issued (not that I bear the gentleman any ill will). This nondefensive word said, I trust it is established that my speeding isn't worrisome. Rather, my problem is stopping and sitting and waiting on the driver in front of me who hasn't realized the light turned green, or my longsuffering toward that super-cautious nut-job up there who doesn't know that a right turn can be made at this intersection. Though I'd never honk (but why *isn't* there a "soft" honk to use occasionally for gentle encouragement?), I have been known to offer genteel, oral admonitions to slow-pokes to haul their chassis through an intersection.

So, I confess I am not a good waiter. But I doubt that I am alone in this. Impatience comes easier to most of us, being arguably a trait learned in our infancy when we discovered that with just an ear-splitting wail we could command immediate attention, if not relief, from all our distresses. Hence, we who are long past infancy now find it maddening to wait an entire hour for a potato to bake when that potato can be on our plate in five minutes via a microwave oven. Having become accustomed from infancy through adulthood to instant gratification, waiting is a hurdle for us—and learning to wait well is Mount Everest. But waiting, and waiting well, are intrinsic to lively hope.

When scripture says it is good for us to wait quietly for the salvation of the Lord, it is talking about hope, even if it doesn't use the word. But it is speaking about a special quality of waiting, not just a twiddle-your-thumbs, killing of time. It is talking about waiting well. There is a difference. Learning to handle sluggish traffic or baking potatoes is only one kind of waiting, a waiting that summons you to deal with the inflated self-importance that resents any encroachment upon your desires, any "waste" of your time. This, of course, is a worthwhile challenge for anyone's maturity, but it is only a gateway to the deeper challenge of waiting well.

Waiting well requires more because it is about more than momentary delays; it is about purpose-filled, useful waiting. Waiting well is the hoper's crucial essential. It summons us to use the fallow time, to let deep call unto deep and to explore and acquaint ourselves with resources possibly useful for tomorrow's tasks. It redeems the time by divining strategies and dreaming dreams, and by entering a silence in which the soul's roots grow more quietly than the turning of the calendar's pages. To outward observers, those who wait well may appear to be as quiescent as a duck gliding across serene waters. But it is not so; there is no passivity or inactivity here. Beneath the surface, significant labor is transpiring. Its other name is hope.

Every longed-for victory of hope is hammered out on this hard anvil of waiting well. One thinks of Martin Luther King Jr. writing a "Letter from Birmingham Jail" on toilet tissue and around the margins of a *New York Times*, explaining *Why We Can't Wait* any longer; or of his "I Have a Dream" speech asking America to honor the "bad check" it had given the Negro a century earlier.

The Old Testament says this through related and interchangeable Hebrew words for waiting and hoping. An example is Isaiah 8:17 where, in a time of God's seeming absence from Israel, the prophet declares: "I will wait for the LORD who is hiding his face from the house of Jacob, and I will hope in him." The Hebrew word "wait" used in the first phrase connotes simply the passing of time, but the word translated as "hope" in the last phrase is a hybrid of Hebrew words meaning "tension" and "the measuring cord when it is to stretched to its full extent." So, the waiting Isaiah means is more than simply the idle passage of time, it is the "strained expectation"[1] of waiting well.

Another Hebrew word sometimes translated as hope is also frequently translated as "to look to." For example, in Psalm 145:15 we read: "The eyes of all look to you, and you give them their food in due season." The image is of small, nested creatures waiting for a parent to return "in due season" from foraging, bearing tonight's supper. So, Israel's many long experiences of waiting led her to liken waiting well to a measuring tape stretched tight or to the feeling of an empty tummy. This is the torturous side of hope; this is what waiting well can feel like.

Enduring the slow passage of time under the stress of unfulfilled dreams is hope's toughest assignment. Often, hope is nothing less than marching toward a far horizon in the service of a sometimes-silent God.

I do not know how many years it took God to create a habitable planet for humankind. Geologists say it took so many centuries that my imagination freezes trying to comprehend such eons. How many million years did it take to carve the Grand Canyon? And then have the human creature float his garbage down its river and fight over its water rights? And watch these self-important two-legged creatures rape and kill, bully and swagger, deceive one another and destroy so many patiently made expressions of God's artistry? "Sometimes I think that patience is one of the great characteristics that distinguishes God from man," wrote Howard Thurman. "God knows how to wait dynamically; everybody else is in a hurry." But Thurman went on to say that patience is only partially concerned with waiting: "it includes also the quality of relentlessness, ceaselessness, and constancy. It is a mood of deliberate calm that is the distilled result of confidence."[2]

As I write these words, the last hours of 2020 are staggering to their end. For most Americans it has been the most stressful year imaginable. The meanest political season in modern American history has been endured, and the end is not in sight. Who knows how long it will take to heal the gashes in public trust we have sustained? A still uncontrolled virus has claimed hundreds of thousands of lives, and though a vaccine has now been produced, it is unclear when and even if enough people will avail themselves of it. Also, the viciousness of embedded racism in our society has again been exposed, but one wonders if even this year's uprisings will dislodge the reign of white supremacy. There is no certain timetable for that victory, even as there is no assurance when a 2020 economy, which made billionaires of a few and threw millions of others to the financial gutter, will be reset in fairness. For all these victories we wait. But that waiting must be infused with the actions of hope—with the depth assignments of meditating, soul-searching, donating, centering, rejoicing, studying, and praying—and the surface tasks of lobbying, protesting, modeling, encouraging, organizing, pestering, and resisting. Only by doing this, do we wait well. To wait otherwise is worse than "wasting" time; it is damning proof of inexcusable indifference.

Ibram X. Kendi concludes his stirring *How to Be An Antiracist* with a sobering confession that he sees nothing in our world today, in our history, "giving me hope that one day antiracists will win the fight, that one day the flag of antiracism will fly over a world of equity." Nevertheless, he persists, held fast by the conviction that "once we lose hope, we are guaranteed to lose." So, he labors on, against all odds, to "give humanity a chance to one day survive, a chance to live in communion, a chance to be forever free."[3] Black preacher Augustus Jones Jr. spoke of that chance in these words: "When you give up before you give out," he said, "you're a goner. You have died before your death. There's no faith to be fired, no hope to kindle, no song to sing, and no prayer to be prayed. God is left with nothing to work with."[4]

Off the northwestern tip of the state of Washington there are a number of small islands that are barely within the United States. Their surrounding waters flow into the Haro Strait, a narrow strip of North-South oriented water that soon feeds into the Pacific Ocean. The rapid flow of cold, deep water through Haro Strait and its fierce tricky tides are well-known and well-respected by the local residents. Annie Dillard spent summers up there and befriended a gifted painter who was experimenting with various papers and canvasses for his paintings. Upon returning to the island one summer, she asked how his work was coming. Rather than answer, he began telling her a story about one of the islanders, Ferrar Burn.

One evening Burn saw a log floating in the channel. From what he could tell the log was yellow, as in the yellow Alaskan cedar so prized by locals for building. One of the desirable qualities of this Alaskan cedar is its density, but that also means it is heavy in the water and scavenging one of those logs usually requires a motorboat. But Ferrar set out, rowing his little skiff, and soon joyfully confirmed the log was indeed the valued Alaskan cedar and also short enough, barely eight feet, that he was sure he could hook onto it and row back to shore while the tide was still slack.

He slipped his chain through the iron staple hammered into one end of the log by the upstream logger who had lost it and began rowing homeward. He had barely begun his return trek, however, when the tide changed. The waters caught the log and tugged it southward toward the ocean. Nonetheless, Ferrar kept rowing north toward home. It was futile. His rowing was no match for the power of the tide dragging the heavy log and him south and out to sea. As the sun set, Ferrar could see he had been swept southward the full length of the island even though he had never ceased rowing in the opposite direction. When the moon rose, he saw only a sparse stretch between him and the wide sea. Nevertheless, he kept rowing toward home.

Finally, he sensed the tide go slack—and begin to come in again. The current reversed! Ferrar continued rowing, but now he felt the power of the northbound waters dragging the heavy log and him homeward. It was as though they were being carried like platters across the surface of the water. By three o'clock in the morning Ferrar was back to his island's southern tip. As dawn broke, he finally pulled the log up onto the beach by his cabin. His wife, wondering where he'd been all night, saw him tugging it ashore.

The painter who told Dillard the story said: "I saw him a few days later. Everybody knew he'd been carried out almost to Stuart Island, trying to bring in a log. Everybody knew he just kept rowing in the same direction. I asked him about it. He said he had a little backache. I didn't see the palms of his hands."

Then the painter added: "You asked how my work is going. That's how it's going. The current's got me. Feels like I'm about in the middle of the channel now. I just keep at it. I just keep hoping the tide will turn and bring me in."[5]

Those who hope, row, and wait for the tide to turn.

NOTES

[1]Hans Walter Wolff, *Anthropology of the Old Testament,* trans. Margaret Kohl (Philadelphia: Fortress Press, 1974), 150.

[2]Howard Thurman, *Deep Is the Hunger: Meditations for Apostles of Sensitiveness* (New York: Harper & Brothers, 1951), 53, 54.

[3] X. Kendi, *How to Be an Antiracist* (New York: One World, 2019), 238. William Sloane Coffin in 1993 wrote that there were "plenty of reasons to be pessimistic about our immediate future…But the political climate can and may well change. And in the meantime, if not optimistic, we can be hopeful, hope being a state of mind independent of the state of the world. If faith puts us on the road, hope is what keep us there. It enables us to keep a steady eye on remote ends. It makes us persistent when we can't be optimistic, faithful when results elude us. For like nothing else in the world, hope arouses a passion for the possible, a determination that our children not be asked to shoulder burdens we let fall." *A Passion for the Possible: A Message to U.S. Churches* (Louisville, KY : Westminster John Knox Press, 1993), 3.

[4]William Augustus Jones Jr. *Responsible Preaching and Twenty Other Sermons* (Morristown, NJ: Aaron Press, 1989), 86.

[5]Annie Dillard, *The Writing Life* (New York: Harper & Row, 1989), ch. 6.

Where to Look for Hope

We were being pounded by the storm so violently that on the next day they began to throw the cargo overboard, and on the third day with their own hands they threw the ship's tackle overboard. When neither sun nor stars appeared for many days, and no small tempest raged, all hope of our being saved was at last abandoned.

(Acts 27:18-20)

In a hotel room in Quito, Ecuador, Annie Dillard says she read one night from a Gideon Bible for twenty minutes before a double-edged razor blade slid from its pages.[1] She wrote nothing about her reaction. But then, her reaction isn't what's important; the story behind that razor blade is what is important.

We can, of course, fabricate a story about a businessperson or a politician or even a priest for whom all the scripts have been played out. Nothing is left. No door remains open. Except the door to a rented room in a nameless hotel where sweet relief awaits through self-destruction.

But before any of us seeks that room, there are the little deaths that lead there…the little deaths we all face and feel and weep over. The jobs that didn't pan out, the love that got away, the kid who took your best and then spat in your face, the blow-up any fool should have seen coming, the offer that was too good to be true and viciously proved it, the handsome face and slim figure that turned old and puffy, the financial future that never happened. These are the little deaths that cry out day after day for the healing touch of hope. And if they fail to find it, well…

Besieged by little deaths, where are we to look for hope? One place I want to explore is a story about a commanding general of the Syrian army whose name was Naaman. According to the record (2 Kgs. 5:1-14), he was internationally known and highly respected. But Naaman was a leper. He suffered from a malady that disfigured him and mandated a fear-filled, arm's-length life far worse than any "social distancing" we have known.

Among the servants within Naaman's home, however, there was a young girl who served his wife as a maid. We do not know her name; all we know is that she was an Israelite who had been brought to Syria as a spoil of one of Naaman's battles. One day this little one remarked: "If only my LORD were with the prophet who is in Samaria, he would cure him of his leprosy."

Naaman overheard her words and immediately rushed to his king, reporting the girl's statement. And the king, eager to have his general cured of the foul disease, promptly gave him permission to go and find this prophet; he even wrote a letter to Israel's king requesting his cooperation, loading Naaman's entourage with lavish thank-you gifts for that assistance. But Naaman presented the king with the letter, he was distraught—he had no idea where any such "faith healer" was to be found. So, Naaman's hopes suffered yet another little death and the story might have ended there had not Elisha, "the prophet who is in Samaria," heard of the meeting.

Elisha contacted the king, telling him to send the afflicted general to him. But when Naaman and all his chariots arrived at Elisha's house, the prophet did not go out to greet or speak with him. Instead, he sent a messenger to instruct Naaman to go wash in the Jordan River seven times, promising that when he did so "your flesh shall be restored and you shall be clean." Receiving this reception and command, Naaman exploded: "I thought that for me he would surely come out and stand and call on the name of the LORD his God, and would wave his hand over the spot, and cure the leprosy! Are not Abana and Pharpar, the rivers of Damascus, better than all the rivers of Israel? Could I not wash in them and be clean?"

Once again, a little death cloaked Naaman. But as he started to storm away from yet another disappointed hope, his servants spoke calmly to him. "Father, if the prophet had commanded you to do something difficult, would you not have done it? How much more, when all he said to you was, 'Wash, and be clean'?"

Brought up short by that question, Naaman reconsidered and "went down and immersed himself seven times in the Jordan, according to the word of the man of God; his flesh was restored like the flesh of a young boy, and he was clean."

Here is a beautiful story about hope being answered with healing. But it is also a story of surprise, for its plot-turning, hope-giving moments come mostly from unknowns. Although a ton of testosterone struts across the stage of this story—two kings, a military commander, even a high-profile "faith healer"— the catalyst for most of their movements comes from characters whose names aren't even on the playbill.

First, there is the unnamed servant girl. Though she has been abducted from her parents and homeland by the very general whose wife she now serves, she is the one who awakens Naaman's hopes. This story's happy ending begins with a mistreated, nameless nobody who shows herself to be a gracious somebody.

Then there are the servants of Naaman. When he rages over Elisha's discourteous reception and humbling River Jordan instructions, it is Naaman's unnamed servants who calm their master and turn him from angry disappointment to shouts of joy.

The hope-bringers in this tale are not the powerful or the famous. They are the persons whose names no one bothered to record. Adding to the surprise, their story is told within a biblical book titled "The Book of Kings." So, slipped into this official record of the antics and accomplishments of royalty, there is the memory that now and again it was the "ignorables" who made the difference. It's a quiet confession that though the "great" ones have their needed place, hope is not just in them. Our hope is also in the ones Google doesn't recognize.

The hope we seek is often offstage among the understudies. It is in the everyday folks who, like this little girl, display uncommon compassion. It's in the quiet ones such as these servants who have wisdom to lend. It's in the bold ones who absurdly tackle huge problems with bite-size endeavors. For instance, a friend of mine, living in West Africa, became alarmed by the loss of life to malaria. So he began privately raising money to purchase and give away insecticide-treated mosquito nets.

Up against the widespread devastation of malaria his puny mom-and-pop effort seemed ludicrous. But sixteen years later when his work called him elsewhere, he'd distributed some 200,000 nets. The World Health Organization estimates each net saves two lives. Not bad for one man with no medical training up against a deadly disease. I consider this a sign of hope.

Or, to bring it nearer to where we live, consider these situations: Somewhere near you two persons of different colored skins are tackling racism by making determined efforts to befriend one another. There's a lady providing TLC in her home for kids caught in "the system." And a fellow is volunteering two nights a week teaching some of America's twenty-plus million illiterate adults to read. Signs of hope are they all. Perhaps you are one of them.

And then there's the lad who, when he learned about world hunger, began knocking on neighborhood doors for donations. When someone asked if he thought he was going to cure the problem all by himself, he said: "Nah, my friend Billy's working on the other side of the street." Watch that kid; he too is a sign of hope.

Speaking of kids, how about whispering a prayer every time you drive by a school? Inside those walls, minds are being filled with knowledge, imaginations are being stirred, creativity is being encouraged. Unheralded teachers are going about their "ignorable" role, molding tomorrow's scientists, business leaders, parents, and pastors. In every lab and physics formula, in every classroom, there's a sign of hope.

A man of eighty-four, his wife having died six months before and their only child living half a continent away, was puzzled when his front doorbell rang one afternoon. He hadn't opened that door since the last funeral guest left. But upon opening it, he saw a barely-known neighbor on his porch, a home-cooked meal in hand. "Just wanted you to know, we been thinkin' about you," was the giver's only and awkward sentence as he handed over the meal. In every act of kindness, there is a sign of hope.

Sometimes congregations get so enamored with their superstar preacher, they forget the greater treasure they have in the unheralded every-Sunday attenders, pray-ers, tithers, huggers, workers, and listeners. In automotive terms, they need to learn that the church runs on regular. In every pew, a sign of hope.

Another big surprise in the Naaman story is his discovery that the god of a defeated enemy might be the source of his healing. To understand this, one must remember that in Naaman's day each kingdom had its own god, and if a kingdom lost a war, its god was understood to have been beaten also. Thus, for Naaman to seek help from a representative of a defeated nation was a stunning act—and all the more so when that unlikely god proved to be a merciful, healing God even for a foreign man of war. You never know where the hammer, nails, and glue of hope may be found.

For instance, when it was rumored that Israel's hoped-for messiah had been found in the dinky, no-place of Nazareth, one listener skeptically, prejudicially asked: "Can anything good come from Nazareth?" (John 1:46). I can understand that response; it's still easy to write off the Nazarene as an "ignorable." Even some of the folks who jabber most about him ignore most everything he taught. And to this day many spit out his name as nothing more than a meaningless profanity. But it is also true that for two thousand years millions of people have sung his name in gut-deep, grateful praise. Some have groaned it, even screamed it in loving appeal when they could utter nothing more, and multitudes have whispered his name as their last word—finding in this nobody from Nazareth the hope their soul so desperately sought. Where might we look for hope? Why not try looking to Jesus?

I believe that among taken-for-granted, ignorable people, and from places and ideas and movements on few radar screens, there are resources we are foolish to ignore. And books need to be on this list too. Certainly, the Bible should be, for as one of its writings says, through "the encouragement of the scriptures we…have hope" (Rom. 15:4). Admittedly, in some patches the Bible can be drier than the Mojave, but for those who persevere, the hope of the universe begins to come into view.

William James left this memorable testimony about where he looked for hope: "I am done with great things and big things, great institutions and big success, and I am for those tiny, invisible molecular moral forces that work from individual to individual, creeping through the crannies of the world like so many rootlets, or like the capillary oozing of water, yet which if you give them time, will rend the hardest monuments of man's pride."[2]

Before the days when soldiers were equipped with night-vision goggles, I'm told they were trained to look just to the left of where they thought the desired target or object might be. That little adjustment helped the eye to detect what direct viewing obscured. There may be spiritual truth in that maneuver. We may see hope best if we cease looking only at where we think hope ought to be and begin to pay attention to the actions and the people on the margins. Like seeds in the ground, or babies in the womb, or Jesus in the tomb, hope arises from dark places.[3]

The Bible verses that introduced this meditation tell of some storm-besieged sailors who abandoned all hope. Who can blame them? They had been trained to steer by the sun and the stars, not by listening to the counsel of prisoners shackled below deck. In this instance, however, the prisoner was the Apostle Paul, an unrecognized saint of God, an ambassador of Jesus. Fortunately, when these sailors shifted their attention from the angry clouds above them to the little man before them, they "all were brought safely to land" (Acts 27:44b).

Remember that razor blade? The fact that it was still within that Bible, unused, permits me to hope that its owner had found within an often-scorned, cheap hotel Bible, a phrase, a sentence, or a story that quieted a frantic heart. Maybe, for just a moment, that frantic heart, too long drowning in sadness, looked up and realized that Another had also entered that room, bringing grace and truth and hope. We can hope.

NOTES

[1]Annie Dillard, *For the Time Being* (New York: Vintage Books, 1999), 138.

[2]Though attributed to William James, this quote's precise source remains elusive. I first saw it in Wayne E. Oates, *The Psychology of Religion* (Waco, TX: Word Books, 1973).

[3]Barbara Brown Taylor, *Learning to Walk in the Dark* (New York: HarperOne, 2014), 219.

When God Disappoints

Hope deferred makes the heart sick, but a desire fulfilled is a tree of life.
(Prov. 13:12)

Decades ago, during a Holy Week Bible study, I spent several minutes developing the idea that Jesus' suffering was not restricted to the physical events of that one week; his entire ministry was a spiritual *Via Dolorosa*. I remember being inordinately proud of my observation—right up until "Sally" interrupted me, her voice clear and strong.

I knew of her long, valiant, but unsuccessful struggles against depression and related mental health challenges. Physically and financially, she was a person of wealth, but it was sadly different inside her spirit. And on this night, as I spoke of Jesus' suffering, the usually silent "Sally" blurted out with uncontrollable protest: "But his lasted only three years!" She had hoped for so much more from God.

On another occasion, when I paid a visit to an every-Sunday-attending member of my church, who was dying of cancer, her husband kindly escorted me to the bedroom where she was resting. We visited for a few minutes, but it was clear she had little energy for the visit. I began to make my departure by asking if I might pray with her. Her reply was firm and not painted with any pious lace: "Go ahead and pray if you want to," she said, "but it hasn't done any good so far." She too had hoped for so much more.

Unmet hopes create disillusionment, even a resentment that is deep beyond telling. Yet being disappointed in God is a fact of life for many people. They hear and read wonderful testimonies about what God did for others who trusted and hoped in God. But their own story has no comparable miraculous rescue; no parting seas or visiting angels have come their way. Which means they must continue to endure their pain and bear the additional sorrow of a God who failed.

> I wish, thou know'st, to be resign'd,
> And wait with patient hope;
> But hope delay'd fatigues the mind,
> And drinks the spirit up.[1]

We are back to the question of the trustworthiness of God—for hope is always a matter of confidence in God's goodness—and the issue of how we interpret God's promises. (See "The Grandest Gamble.") So, let's continue the discussion, beginning with further consideration of God's promises.

I have said that hope finds one of its building blocks in the many promises of God, and I pointed specifically to the promise of God to Abraham to be a God working for blessing "for all the families of the earth." The other building block of hope I have named is imagination, or the creative possibilities that can arise from brooding upon the promise-material. Both of these, however, are open to misapplication, and as a consequence each of them may lead us to disappointment with God.

With regard to the misapplication of promise-material, we may be glad that scripture has many promises that are made to God's people throughout the ages. But we also need to remember, however reluctantly, that these promises for us today are "borrowed" promises. Reading the Bible is inherently akin to reading other peoples' mail; we are not the first intended recipients. Thus, we can come upon a promise made to a biblical person in a particular life circumstance and identify so completely with that character that we hear the promise they received as meant for us. Perhaps so. But perhaps not.

Interpreting the Bible necessitates seeing parallels and similarities, but no two cases are clones. In our interpreting we must always respect the integrity of the story and its promise in all its particularities. To imagine, for example, that God's promise to Elijah or to Moses or to Deborah or Mary was actually made to me is always an extension and a possible misapplication of the uniqueness of that promise to that individual. So, we must be careful to hear the promises of God within the scripture at arm's length and to appropriate them as bearing our own name only by hope. We may hope that what once was said pertains to us as well; but it is unwise to recast ourselves as being Elijah or Moses, Deborah or Mary.

A second consideration may be noted in the imagination aspect of hope. Even if we respect the "borrowed" nature of the biblical promise-material, we can go astray in our imagining. Most often this happens by imposing a desired specificity upon a promise that in itself is not that specific. Abraham's imagination might, for example, have gone astray by assuring himself that the "promised land" was going to be arable farmland, or that a "great name" for himself must be that of a king. Rather than let imagination lead him to exploration and discovery of God's intentions, Abraham would thus have converted a general promise into a detailed contract—and set himself up for severe disappointment when God failed to meet his own expectations. Some unmet hopes come from our unwarranted conversion of a promise into a contract that we ourselves crafted and forged God's name upon.

Sometimes even church talk can set us up for this. "The LORD has promised good to me," is a line from the hymn "Amazing Grace" that I noted appreciatively in "Promises and Other Odd-Fathers." This sentence has the full support of all of scripture. It does not need to be "borrowed," since from Abraham onward we may point to the promise that God is working for blessing "for all the families of the earth." A problem arises, however, in a following line of the hymn that declares, as a consequence of God's promised "good," "He will my shield and buckler be." Unfortunately, this line projects into God's promise of "good," the specific of divine protection. Six million Jews lost to German anti-Semitism would challenge the notion that God promises divine protection to anyone. Thus, even a beloved hymn shows us how easy it is to place unwarranted specifics upon promise-material, opening the door to disappointment with God.

A more helpful way to approach specific hopes may be seen in the wisdom of Bryan Stevenson, the Harvard-trained lawyer who through his Equal Justice Initiative has awakened us to the dismaying number of Black men unjustly held in America's prisons. But in his attempts to free these prisoners, Stevenson has met many disappointments. So, when Minnie, the wife of a Black man Stevenson was seeking to have released, said to him, "They've kept him for years. Now it's time they let him go. They have to let him go," Stevenson faced a dilemma. History told him to prepare her for the worst, but compassion demanded he urge her to hope for the best. So, he spoke to Minnie about the importance of hopefulness—not hope with a calendar and demand, but hope as a spirit of hopefulness. This, he says, is "not pie in the sky" stuff, not a preference for optimism or pessimism, but rather "an orientation of the spirit."[2] Without setting itself up for disappointment, this spirit looks to God for unstipulated "good."

Having mentioned the Holocaust, I must admit that the Shoah remains the great problem for anyone who wants to maintain belief in a "good"-working God. The chief rabbi of Jerusalem, Israel Meir Lau, a survivor of Buchenwald, has spoken more fittingly to this than I can.

In his memoir Rabbi Lau says he will go to his grave with unanswered questions about this horror; why he was spared but others, such as his brother, were not. But he quotes with approval the words of the great Hasidic Rabbi Menachem Mendel of Kotsk: "I am not capable of worshiping a God whose every path is clear to me," and Lau adds that "when everything is revealed and understood, that is friendship, not Divinity." Finally, he points to the "thick darkness" that scripture says inhabited the ancient Jerusalem temple's holiest place, the earthly throne of God: "Sometimes the Divine Presence rests within a domain that is hidden, concealed behind a screen of mystery."[3] I am no more satisfied with that resolution of the matter than I am certain Lau is, but if Lau, who experienced that hell on earth can leave the matter there, I think it disrespectful, as a Gentile intruder, to push him farther.

But I do note that Nobel prize winner Elie Wiesel, also a Holocaust survivor who lost family members in the flames, wrote, "I have never renounced my faith in God. I have risen against His justice, protested His silence and sometimes His absence, but my anger rises up within faith and not outside it."[4] Wiesel was only sixteen pages into his two-volume memoirs when the sixty-five-year-old admits "my two favorite words, applicable to every situation, be it happy or bleak" are "and yet." He had seen enough of life to know that no story ends with a period; every story has its "and yet" that calls upon us to "shun resignation, to refuse to wallow in sterile fatalism"[5] and press on to find or create the possible good.

"And yet" I must push further to challenge our assumptions about what constitutes "good." Do we truly know what is "good" for us? Most of us would not consider suffering a possible component of what is "good." But anyone who has paid attention to anything knows that, notwithstanding our dislike of it, suffering has often been the context, if not the source, of much "good."

Beethoven's music seems the sweeter for his deafness, Emily Dickinson's poetry the richer for her aloneness, Nelson Mandela's witness the stronger for his decades in prison, Jesus' life the more amazing for all he endured. Thus, I cannot think that the "good" which God has promised is simply a life without grief or pain or stress. In fact, from my own life's journey I now know that much of the "good" I craved across the years would not have been an aid to my own soul's growth or to the "good" of others. God knows better than I do what is "good" for me.

What then can we rightly expect when we place our hope in God? Claypool[6] believed God's help comes to us in several forms, and if we are to avoid the pitfalls of disappointment, we need to keep the entire spectrum before us. One means of God's coming to our aid, he said, continues to be the possibility of divine intervention, in miraculous rescue. Though such responses are the most problematic for many of us, even Jesus in the Garden of Gethsemane prayed for "this cup" to be removed from him. So, we have good company when we ask for miracles of intervention.

However, a second credible expectation of "good" from God is found "when God moves alongside us and invites us to join forces with him in bringing about a solution to our difficulties." Often, through chapters of our lives that may not have felt "good" at all, we develop skills or insights that in the hour of greatest need become available for collaborative effort with God's powers. "Again and again," Claypool said, "the Holy One invites us to use our own creativity and resourcefulness in finding solutions to our problems. God honors our maturity by asking us to partner with him in collaboration, rather than allowing us to remain in an infantile stance."

A third expression of God's help that we may hope for is the gift of endurance. This occurs when God says: "There will be no solving of the problem, but I will give you the strength to endure the unchangeable and to experience real growth in the process." We would prefer, of course, to have the burden lifted and to mount up with wings like eagles, and miraculously fly away from our problem, or to receive collaborative assistance to run through them and not be weary. But when life and we ourselves are broken, the gift of endurance, the strength to "walk and not faint" (Isa. 40:31) is an exceedingly "good" gift.

I would add a fourth element that is surely assumed within Claypool's three forms of God's help: companionship. It is never wrong to ask God to be "with us." It must please God to be wanted, especially if we place no demands or expectations upon the Holy One. In a late-night movie I once watched, and whose title I cannot now retrieve, an Indian medical doctor sits tearfully with his dying wife. Having exhausted all his medical knowledge, he weeps: "I feel so useless; so helpless. I cannot do a thing!" But his consoling wife desirously whispers: "You can hold my hand." To be held when everything else gives way, is this not one of God's greatest gifts (Ps. 73:23)?

In all these ways—miracle, collaboration, endurance, and companionship—God's help may come to us. It is not easy to "let God be God" as the chooser of the best form of "grace to help in our times of trouble" (Heb. 4:16), but learning to do so enables us to live with hope, a hope that does not disappoint us.

NOTES

[1]William Cowper, H.S. "The Waiting Soul," Hymn XXXIII of Olney Hymns in *The Complete Poetical Works of William Cowper*, ed. Milford (London: Oxford, 1913), 454.

[2]Bryan Stevenson, *Just Mercy* (New York: One World, 2015), 219.

[3]Israel Meir Lau, *Out of the Depths: The Story of a Child of Buchenwald Who Returned Home at Last* (New York: Sterling Publishing, 2020), 2-3.

[4]Elie Wiesel, *All Rivers Run to the Sea: Memoirs* (New York: Alfred A. Knopf, 1995), 84.

[5]Ibid., 16.

[6]John Claypool, "What Can We Expect of God?" in *The Hopeful Heart* (Harrisburg, PA: Morehouse Publishing, 2003), 35-61.

Dare America Speak of Hope?

(Thoughts on Presidential Inauguration Day: January 20, 2021)

He has told you, O mortal, what is good;
and what does the LORD *require of you but to do justice,*
and to love kindness, and to walk humbly with your God?
(Mic. 6:8)

Today, Joseph R. Biden is being sworn in as president of the United States. At such occasions the word "hope" will predictably be bandied about. Political observer Mark Shields says the enduring hallmarks of American politics are pragmatism and optimism. However, I wonder if it is truly helpful to speak today of hope, when toxic animosity saturates every breath we take. Will not hope-talk mask the gravity of the hour and pretend things are not really as ominous as they appear?

America has seen dark hours before. Fort Sumter, Pearl Harbor, and 9/11 are some of the more notable. January 6, 2021, now joins that list. On that day our Capitol was overrun by some supporters of the President of the United States who, refusing to admit his defeat in the presidential election, stirred them to violent protest. Fort Sumter, Pearl Harbor, and 9/11 catapulted us into wars. It is unknown today if January 6, 2021 will mean the same. But the truth is, Americans have been spoiling for a knock-down, drag-out fight with each other for more than a decade.

You need not be brilliant to list the issues that have long been devouring our unity: racism, income inequality, extreme individualism, gender and sexual discrimination, education, immigration, abortion, government's place, health care, climate change, religious favoritism—all these and more found a place along our nation's fault lines. But rather than face these issues dialogically, searching for the common good, our differing opinions became non-negotiable demands. Religious leaders made them sacred dogma, wealthy patrons funded them, eager media sources monetized them, and politicos manned the barricades, ratcheting up the rhetoric to inflamed enmity. Each side judged the other to be morally deficient and/or intellectually inferior, making respectful conversation a hurdle, especially by giving differing meanings to shared terms. Rather than work together, we walked in packs and forsook one another. January 6, 2021 may well be seen as the day our intra-national cold war died. We now are at point-blank in America.

Kurt Anderson begins his sprightly 440-page romp through American history, aptly titled: *Fantasyland: How America Went Haywire: A 500-Year History*, with this observation:

> People tend to regard the Trump moment—this post-truth, alternative facts moment—as some inexplicable and crazy *new* American phenomenon. In fact, what's happening is just the ultimate extrapolation and expression of attitudes and instincts that have made America exceptional for its entire history—and really, from its prehistory.

Unfortunately, after readers wade through Anderson's 400-plus page documentation of this claim and are begging for encouragement and strategies for an exit from our fantasyland, Anderson offers a few "to do" items and limps to his final three words: "We can hope."[1] For many people, hope seems a cruel and airy action plan when facing the meltdown of a nation.

In contrast, there is the sobriety of South African theologian and activist Allan Boesak who asks: "Dare We Speak of Hope?"[2] Boesak is a veteran of the apartheid struggle in his native land and a keen observer of American politics. He has seen hope used as a vital stimulant and also as a wicked ploy; he knows from experience that hopers are fair game for hustlers. So he says we dare speak of hope *only* if we also speak of woundedness, of struggle, of seeking peace, of fragile faith, and of dreaming. In sum, hope-talk must be responsible, holistic talk—or it is suspect and cruel.

Some are suggesting our best hope-talk begins with 2 Chronicles 7:14: "If my people… will humble themselves, pray, seek my face, and turn from their wicked ways, then I will hear from heaven, and will forgive their sin and heal their land." This is a worthy text for consideration, but I don't believe it is the best scriptural word for today. It is an abused and over-used text, too often sermonically used by preachers as a license to lambast their cherry-picked six "wicked ways."

A more useful framework for helpful hope-talk comes from the prophet Micah: "He has told you, O mortal, what is good: and what does the LORD require of you but to do justice, and to love kindness, and to walk humbly with your God?" Here are terms not already slimed over by our polarized rhetoric, a sentence with a breadth of wisdom exceeding our narrow talking points.

We dare to speak of hope only if we do justice.

Reading this, we are mistaken if we assume our understanding of justice is the same as Micah's. Our tradition defines justice as fairness for all; but as noble as our tradition is, it isn't what Micah is talking about. Justice in Micah's understanding was fairness with a plus: a preference for the power-less It included a thumb-on-the-scales concern for the have-nots. Check it out. Whenever prophets such as Micah talk about justice, they point to the cause of the poor. To the prophets, the doing of justice was not simply access to the courts for the poverty-stricken, but favoring them when their case came to trial. The prophets knew the rich would find a way, that if need be, they would even *blast* a way forward. Doing justice meant *making* a way for the powerless to move forward also. The "ignorables," the little guy, must be taken seriously.

Justice says we must mind the concerns of all, not just guard the interests of the dominant race or class. Justice inculcates the concept of "us," *all* of us. And the prophets warn not only of God's judgment but also of the rage and resentment, the societal decay that follows when "me" and "mine" take precedence over "us."

Micah says justice is something to be done; it is not a discussion topic. It is a deed to be done! Hope-talk is only hypocritical halitosis if justice is ignored. But when justice is being sought, lively hope and life together become possible.

We dare to speak of hope only if we love kindness.

Kindness is a counterpart to justice. Whereas justice seems stern, kindness is friendly. Kindness conjures images of soft eyes and generous deeds, unlike the solemnity of the halls of justice. Kindness considers the "other" as a fellow human being, a neighbor rather than an adversary, a companion more than a competitor. Even so, kindness may best be pictured not as the opposite of justice, but as the manner in which justice is to be displayed.

But what does kindness have to do with hope? Perhaps a homely answer comes in the casseroles brought to mourners at a time of loss. The kindness of casseroles brings more than bodily nourishment; it represents social connec-tion, it says care, it brings hope. Perhaps a personal answer may be heard in the soft reply I once received after apologizing for a thoughtless statement I'd made. The kindness of that gentle response was life-giving; it brought hope that our relationship was not dead. In the public arena, kindness is shown by dealing fairly rather than meanly with adversaries and thereby leaving hope's door open. Kindness deletes the "gotcha" lines and the zingers that too easily come to our lips, words that build towering walls for reconciliation to climb. Illustrations could be piled high, but the ultimate example is the kindness of God through which we can find hope for living and even in dying. Kindness softens the sting. It brings healing and hope.

Attention must, however, be paid to Micah's way of stating this. He does not say the requirement is to "be kind," but to "love kindness"—not to admire it from a distance, but to love it. The requirement is to cling to the ideal, to love a way of relating even if for the moment you cannot love the other, the offender, the opponent. The call is to a way of life, one that gives hope a chance to blossom.

We dare to speak of hope only if we walk humbly with God.

Humility is in short supply. Its opposite, community-killing cocksureness, has been rising for years and is now off the charts. If it is not heard in our adamant, albeit differing convictions about the facts of any issue, then it reveals itself in the haughty manner in which we clothe our words and dismiss dissenters as either redneck bigots or America-hating socialists. If we are to find rescuing hope, one essential is the restoration of humility—and its requisite repentance from demonizing other views.

This arrogance reaches its worst when it puts on religious clothing and pretends to know and represent God's will and way down to the fourth decimal point. When this happens, we are not walking humbly with God; we are using God as the patron saint of our opinions. I confess: I have my own opinions and am satisfied they are solidly grounded in biblical, theological, and political wisdom. And I refuse to dismiss our political differences as mere misunderstandings. No, some things are just wrong! But...

A memorable line from the prophet Isaiah says, "All we like sheep have gone astray; we have all turned to our own way" (53:6). That indicting word "all" is twice repeated, and my reluctant observation is that "all" of us—of every political leaning—ignore its pointed finger. Each of us "turns to our own way," that is, to our chosen TV channel or columnist or commentator or preacher as *the* voice of truth and high moral ground. But that "way" leads to death, not to hope. Democracy requires compromise, not crusades.

No one in these United States knows the mind of God on all the divisive issues confronting us. Not the two being sworn in today, Joe Biden and Kamala Harris, nor Franklin Graham, nor William Barber, nor Sean Hannity, nor Alexandria Ocasio-Cortez—not you, and certainly not me. We just don't have the capacity to know the mind of God on all these matters!

But what we do know—because Micah was led by God to tell us—is that God wants to see justice done and kindness loved on earth as in heaven. We know that humility before God and one another is a requisite for the doing of justice and the loving of kindness.

We walk most humbly with God when in humility we ask all God's children to help us find and do justice. We walk most humbly with God when we deal kindly with one another in this quest for justice. When we together pursue justice while loving kindness, we release the rescuing power of the hope we so desperately need.

I have my hopes for what today's change in administrations will bring to America. So do more than 300,000,000 other citizens. But all our hopes ultimately depend upon Micah's kind of "justice for all" and Micah's love of "kindness by all" becoming the mode of this now festering nation. God, help us to do justice and love kindness that good hope might thrive among us.

NOTES

[1]Kurt Anderson, *Fantasyland: How America Went Haywire: A 500-Year History* (New York: Random House, 2017), 11, 440.

[2]Allan Aubrey Boesak, *Dare We Speak of Hope? Searching for a Language of Life in Faith and Politics* (Grand Rapids: Wm. B. Eerdmans Publishing Co., 2014).

Wonders Do Happen!
Regret and Reconciliation

How very good and pleasant it is when kindred live together in unity!
(Ps. 133:1)

The animosity of today's political climate, though alarming, is not unprecedented in America's history. Instances are the fires of the American Civil War, and sixty years earlier when two Founding Fathers, John Adams and Thomas Jefferson, became political enemies. Although the repercussions of both of these tragic events are still very much with us, there is encouragement hidden even within these stories, not-so-well-known aspects of regret and reconciliation found by those at the center of these epic struggles. When we despair of change, there are just enough stories such as these to nourish hope.

To see the other side of the question...

Samuel T. Foster, born in South Carolina in November of 1829, moved when he was eighteen years old with his family to Hallettsville, Texas—midway between Houston and San Antonio. He became a lawyer and in 1860 was appointed the chief justice of Live Oak County, Texas, north of Corpus Christi. The following year Texas joined the Confederacy, and within a year young Judge Foster was mustered into Confederate service as a first lieutenant in the Texas Cavalry. His exemplary leadership as a company commander was rewarded by a promotion to the rank of Captain, but by mid-April of 1865 Foster and his men were encamped near Greensboro, North Carolina, under the command of General Joseph E. Johnson who was then in peace talks with Union General William Sherman near Durham, North Carolina.

Foster's men were aware that the Confederate Capital in Richmond, Virginia, had fallen on April 2; that General Lee had surrendered his army at Appomattox, Virginia on April 9; and that President Lincoln had been assassinated on April 15. But the consequences of these matters were unclear. So, the camp conversations were understandably filled with rumors and fear-based speculations about the soldiers' personal fate. Finally, on Thursday, April 27, General Johnson announced the agreed-upon surrender and its terms. Excerpts from Captain Foster's diary[1] reveal the reactions—and surprising changes of mind—within the minds of some of his men.

Foster notes the "dreadful night" just passed, "all hands up and talking over the situation." His men replay the war again and again, "count up the killed and wounded, then the results obtained" and yield to their grief. "If crying would have done any good, we could have cried all night."

Foster reviews in his mind the beginning of the war and visualizes "the young men in the bloom of life—the flower of the country," who volunteered "to defend their country from the Yankee hosts, who were coming to desolate their homes." They shut down their stores and warehouses, put aside their plows and axes, and fell in line to defend their country. But now, "where are they?" Foster recalls the men in his own company and regiment and brigade whose bodies were maimed, whose lives were lost in battles in Arkansas, at Chickamauga and Missionary Ridge, at Atlanta and Franklin and Nashville: "noble men" in whom there was "no cooling down, no tapering off, no lukewarmness."

And "who is to blame for all this waste of human life," he asks. "And what does it amount to? Has anything been gained by all this sacrifice? What were we fighting for, the principles of slavery?" Then comes his solemn admission: "And now the slaves are all freed, and the Confederacy has to be dissolved. We have to go back into the Union. Ah! there is the point. Will there ever be any more Union, as there once was?"

Foster notes the "men still talking politics, but it is over and over the same thing, with the same regrets for our loss, and ends with the same What does it amount to?"

Later in the day talk begins "about going home, by what route, and whether we will have to walk all the way [to Texas]." "Our guns," he says, "have all been turned in, to our own Ordnance officers. And we suppose to save us from further humiliation there has not been a Yank in sight of us yet."

Foster's entry provides no information about camp activities, but it does record a stunning development in the minds of his men: "It seems curious that mens [sic] minds can change so sudden, from opinions of life long, to new ones a week old. I mean that men who have not only been taught from their infancy that the institution of slavery was right; but men who actually owned and held slaves up to this time,—have now changed in their opinion regarding slavery, so as to be able to see the other side of the question,—to see that for man to have property in man was wrong, and that the "Declaration of Independence meant more than they had ever been able to see before. That all men are, and of right ought to be free" has a meaning different from the definition they had been taught from their infancy up—and to see that the institution (though perhaps wise) had been abused, and perhaps for that abuse this terrible war with its results was brought upon us as a punishment. These ideas come not from the Yanks or northern people but come from reflection, and reasoning among ourselves."

Perhaps unconsciously indicating the immensity of this reappraisal, Foster's diary tells us nothing of particular notice for three days. And then this:

May 4th

"We are getting accostomed [sic] to the new order of things," he writes, "but there is considerable speculation as to what will be done with us...." "Nearly every one deplores the death of Lincoln and believes that he would have been the best man for us now. That things would have been different if he had lived." Finally, Foster registers this revelation: "Some go so far as to say that perhaps we were wrong, and that the negroes ought to have been freed at the start off...."

While I breathe I shall be your friend

From the beginning their friendship was an improbable affair. John Adams was eight years older than Thomas Jefferson, as pudgy as Jefferson was lanky, and as working-class as Jefferson was an aristocrat. One was of New England Puritan stock, the other born to southern intellectualism. One was a plain, if not dowdy, curmudgeon; the other an elegant gentleman of refinement. Adams was an irrepressible fountain of words—many ungoverned by tact—while Jefferson was the consummate listener who chose his words with great care, attempting never to need to mend the fences Adams bulldozed without ever noticing. Yet the two immediately became good friends when the thirty-two-year-old Virginian entered Adams' Continental Congress world of 1774.

Jefferson was "so prompt, frank, explicit, and decisive, that he soon seized upon my heart," said Adams.[2] When the moment called for a formal Declaration of Independence to be drawn up, Adams favored Jefferson as the wordsmith and upon reviewing the product gave it hearty approval.

When the winds of war were spent, their friendship deepened as both served as deputies of the new United States to France and England. Adams' wife, Abigail, befriended the lonely Virginian, often inviting him to the family's table, and helping him grieve when news came of the death of his two-year-old daughter back in Virginia. Abigail urged him to have his older daughter join him in Paris, and when nine-year-old Polly arrived, Abigail all but adopted Jefferson's daughter as her own. Adams and Jefferson talked politics into the late hours of night; they toured Europe's historic sites together. But then they returned to the cauldron of the United States of America.

Some historians characterize the 1790s political environment reentered by these two as "the Age of Passion," for it was a "decade-long shouting match" of "shrill accusatory rhetoric, flamboyant displays of ideological intransigence, intense personal rivalries, and hyperbolic claims of imminent catastrophe."[3] Sadly, the Adams-Jefferson friendship foundered within this storm. Publically (and stated simplistically), their division stemmed from Adams' commitment to a strong Federal government and Jefferson's insistence upon what might later be called "states' rights." But privately, the wounds that were given and received by each from the other, and the others' supporters, were deep and not easily dismissed as just politics.

Adams, always the more thin-skinned of the two, was especially offended by Jefferson's tactics in 1799 when Jefferson, as Adams' vice president, ran against and eventually defeated Adams in the presidential election. Before dawn on Jefferson's inauguration day, Adams boarded a stagecoach for the 500-mile trek to his Quincy, Massachusetts home, a forlorn sixty-five-year-old titan exiting the stage into bitter retirement. There was no reason to expect the two would ever again speak to one another.

Twelve smoldering years of silence passed, years in which Jefferson served two terms (1800–1808) as president and then retired to Monticello, generally as admired as Adams was rejected. Only once in those years was the silence broken—by Abigail Adams. In 1805 Jefferson's daughter Polly, beloved by Abigail while in Europe, died of complications in childbirth, and Abigail, grieved by her death, wrote a sympathy note to Jefferson. Reading more into the letter than he should, Jefferson replied as though all was now forgotten and forgiven, but Abigail, incensed by his presumption, fired back an accusatory rebuke, and, with that, the stony curtain of silence again separated the former friends.

In 1811, finally, a mutual friend of both men and their colleague in the revolutionary deliberations thirty-seven years before, Dr. Benjamin Rush, began urging a rapprochement upon the two. In monthly letters to both, Rush suggested to each that they write the other, hinting (somewhat inaccurately) that their counterpart was eager for such. To Adams he said: "I consider you and [Jefferson] as the North and South Poles of the American Revolution. Some talked, some wrote, and some fought to promote and establish it but you and Mr. Jefferson *thought* for us all." Rush's cajoling ultimately bore fruit. On January 1, 1812, Adams hazarded a short, initial letter to Jefferson—and Jefferson replied.

In a subsequent letter Adams boldly said: "You and I ought not to die before we have explained ourselves to each other." Thus began a fourteen-year correspondence between the two, yielding a total of 158 letters of self-explanation, inquiry, defense, regret, candor, argument, recollection, and admiration. Their differing political orientations remained intact but were respectfully expressed, each knowing from their personal and political wounds how much easier it had been to dissolve a union than to create a new one.

Today the Adams-Jefferson letters are "generally regarded as the intellectual capstone to the achievements of the revolutionary generation and the most impressive correspondence between prominent statesmen in all of American history."[4] But this verdict is rendered not just for the insight they provide into the political calculations of these men, or for their literary caliber. This correspondence is valued for what it says about the character of the correspondents. Their appreciation for one another was too large to let their differences divide them forever.

And thus, they grew old together. Abigail died in 1818. In June of 1821 Jefferson pensively confided that looking back on life was "like looking over a field of battle. All, all are dead: and ourselves left alone amidst a new generation whom we know not, and who know not us." Adams was of a similar mind, although, as he wrote in 1825: "I look back with rapture to those golden days when Virginia and Massachusetts lived and acted together like a band of brothers," adding a remarkable pledge: "While I breathe I shall be your friend." On the golden anniversary of the Declaration of Independence, July 4, 1826, both men died within five hours of each other, Jefferson's name appreciatively on Adams' dying lips.

***

Winston Churchill, a keen student of history, is on record as saying "the future is unknowable, but the past should give us hope." Erik Larson, writing of Churchill's life and times, added another observation: "History is a lively abode, full of surprises."[5] Reviewing the second thoughts and regret Captain Foster's Texas cavalrymen expressed so quickly, and the reconciliation Jefferson and Adams worked so diligently to achieve, it is difficult not to feel surprise and to hear our frequent cynicism challenged. But these stories from yesterday prove nothing. What they do accomplish is to open a door for our imaginations to play with what might be in our own time. Those whose hope is in God, have reason to look for surprises even now, having learned that God's other name is "Surprise."

NOTES

[1] *The Civil War: The Final Year Told by Those Who Lived It*, ed. Aaron Sheehan-Dean (New York: Penguin Group, 2014), 711-719.

[2] Adams' early assessment is included in a letter of August, 1822, written to Thomas Pickering and cited in Gordon S. Wood, *Friends Divided: John Adams and Thomas* Jefferson (New York: Penguin Press, 2017), 105.

[3] Joseph J. Ellis, *Founding Brothers: The Revolutionary Generation* (New York: Alfred Knopf, 2000), 16.

[4] Ibid., 223.

[5] Erik Larson, *The Splendid and the Vile* (New York: Crown, 2020), xii.

Taste and See, Nibble and Sip

The LORD *of hosts will make for all people a feast of rich food,*
a feast of well-aged wines.
(Isa. 25:6a)

It was just a white J.C. Penney bedsheet, but we handled it with all the care of Marines folding a U.S. flag at a military funeral. *We* in this case was the chairman of the deacons and me, the nineteen-year-old pastor of the Walker Baptist Church. And the reason the two of us were so carefully folding this sheet before the twenty-odd worshipers in front of us was because this was Communion Sunday.

For the past hour the sheet had been draped over the Communion table, no doubt resembling an undertaker's corpse-covering to outsiders' eyes. But we who knew, knew that underneath this sheet were symbols of the body and blood of Jesus. And this sheet had been spread across the table, just as many of us did at home, to protect edibles from flies or other unclean critters in this windows-open, non-air-conditioned room.

Our songs had been sung, the sermon preached, the offering taken, and the announcements made. It was now time for our twice-a-year observance of the LORD's Supper. So, the deacon and I gently lifted and folded the bedsheet so lovingly positioned only an hour earlier by ladies of the church. We laid it aside, the deacon took his seat, I opened and read the prescribed words from my new *Pastor's Manual*, spoke the sincere prayers of thanks of our little group, and then we all ate—crackers and juice. Crackers and juice!

The prophet Isaiah, however, had foreseen a day when the God of heavenly armies would spread a feast of rich foods and fine wines for all people. Hearing that as a little boy, and as the child of teetotaling parents, the idea of God serving up wines (plural!) was shocking, but the always hungry boy within me paid more attention to the rich foods part—and he remembered it now as he stared at his cracker and juice.

In those early years I had learned from various gospel songs about "the marriage supper of the Lamb" slated for heavenly consumption (Rev. 19:5, 9). That also sounded scrumptious, especially when I recalled being a ring bearer at Sally Biggs' wedding where they had a fantastic all-you-can-eat buffet. And now, even as a rookie reverend, I already knew that the original Last Supper had at least been a genuine supper before it became a "holy" meal. So, I keenly felt the disappointing gap between the Bible's depictions of a lip-smacking feast and this semi-annual "supper" of flavorless, hard-as-a-brick "crackers" from the Baptist Book Store, and a single sip of Welch's grape juice.

This was my introduction to what biblical scholars call the "already but not yet" mindset of the Christian faith. It's a part of the "Two Time Zone" concept I discuss in another meditation. In brief, the idea is that the reign of God which Jesus inaugurated among us is really here, but it is also still to come. *Already* it is present, *but not yet* is it fully present. Speaking in the terms of the preceding paragraphs, the feast has already begun, but for the two-thousand-year-time-being we are restricted to the appetizers, juice and crackers. It's a sizable stretch, in the menu and the meaning, but that's the general idea.

Another example is the gift of the Holy Spirit. Old Testament prophecy said the Holy Spirit was to be a part of "last days" phenomena (Joel 2:28, Ezek. 36:25-27). But a month or so after Jesus' resurrection, this "last day" gift was shockingly poured out on the disciple community (Acts 2:14ff). So, Paul said this *already*-given Spirit was a down payment, a "first installment" of our future participation in the Spirit; that is, we have *not yet* received all of God's intention (2 Cor. 1:22; see also Eph. 1:13ff). Paul uses the same both/ and pattern in Romans 8:14-16, where he says that because of the Spirit's presence we *already* "have received the spirit of adoption" (v. 15) and even dare to call upon God as "Abba" (an Aramaic term of endearment, close in meaning to our "Daddy"). But then Paul goes on to say (v. 23) that we "who have the first fruits of the Spirit, groan inwardly while we *wait* for adoption."

"Already but not yet" means that due to God's gracious generosity, gifts that properly belong to tomorrow are being "leaked" ahead of time. The glorious future has been brought into the now! We have *already* been given a foretaste of God's extravagant future, *but* the lip-smacking full menu is *not yet* ours to enjoy. For the time being we are nibblers and sippers, anticipators of the feast being prepared. We live on juice and crackers.

And, of course, you recognize that my meaning here is not a matter of food but of hope. Because we have tasted the powers of the age to come, we want more. We yearn for a greater closeness to God and for a better relationship with all God's children and world. We ache for the injustices of the present to be set right—right now. We've seen a smidgeon of God's better tomorrow, and we want everyone to see the same vision and to help in implementing it from shore to shore. Our appetites have been whetted, but for the present we must "wait well," making do with nibbles and sips, with partial and momentary victories of tomorrow's world.

For some people this isn't enough. For them the gap between our crumbs and our feast talk is just too great. They look at the omnipresent, smothering injustice of our society and put it up against the likelihood of nibblers and sippers or our "slow God" making any dent in it—and shake their heads in disbelief. Our pantry is too empty, our table too bare. As a Black church-friend wearily said during the summer of George Floyd's murder, "Nothing's going to change. There'll be all this fuss and feathers, but then it's gonna go right back to how it's always been." The juice and crackers of waiting-well hope is simply not enough for this sufferer.

A variant of this is visible in those who, despite their Sunday talk, put their truest hope in hardball politics rather than in the church's menu of hope. They conclude that crackers and juice are fine enough for the hereafter, but for here and now, politics is the better bet. The ballot box yields real clout with immediate results! This is a tempting trail because civic responsibility is surely an essential part of Christian discipleship. But it is not a substitute for it. The yearning expressed within our silent supper of crackers and juice has outlived the rise and fall of two thousand years of political change; it remains the nurturing center and quiet judge of all our actions, including our politics.

But then there are also those who are quite happy with this menu. They like the dainty, innocuous cleanliness of it. These are the satisfied, the comfortable who suffer no motivating hungers or thirsts. Their life is secure; they have no beef with any oppressor nor are they bothered by visions of a better world, for their world is already quite nice. Hope for them has become a tiny "me and mine" circle, the center of which is frequent reassurances of an even happier life in heaven.

Finally, thank God, there also those whose spirit feels the gnawing ache for a more just society, for a nation and a world that look more like "thy kingdom come" than scenes from a madhouse. These are the hopers who have the potential to lift the low ceiling of our moderated hopes and who model a different, better tomorrow today. These are the dreamers who live on the "already but not yet" diet of hope. Peering into Sunday's cup, they see more than juice: they see God's blood-red resolve to renew the whole cosmos. Cradling that tacky little cracker in their hands, they see bread from heaven—warm and fresh from Archangel Gabriel's oven, lathered with butter and jam. For them, "taste and see" isn't just a Bible phrase (Ps. 34:8); it is what happens at the LORD's table. As they "taste," they really do "see" the invisible. And they go out and make it visible!

And they also see that they are called to live as family with the *unconvinced* who have ditched any hope, and with the *complicit* who prefer power over hope, and with the *comfortable* whose hope is only about themselves. Yes, all these are within Sunday's Nibble and Sip Fellowship! For true hopers know it is a hollow errand to champion world peace if you can't live in peace with your own family.

Which brings me back to Walker Baptist Church and the two dozen of us gathered in our Sunday best in the noonday heat of an Oklahoma July. Over there is Mrs. Stanton, our blind pianist. She's been a widow for decades and blind for almost as long, but I've never known her to be absent or to botch one note of the three dozen hymns she knows by heart.

Mr. and Mrs. Nichols usually bring Mrs. Stanton to church. He's the deacon chairman, a plumber on weekdays—a good man who overlooks my biblical ignorance and departures from "the true faith" as evidence of my youth. Fortunately, Mrs. Nichols has a softness in her eyes that assures me she'll likely calm him down if ever I cross the line. She's good friends (who am I kidding, everyone knows most everything about everybody in this part of the county!) with Mrs. Tripp, or Ethel, as everyone calls her.

Ethel lives within sight of the church building. In fact, she and her husband Sherwood gave the land on which this church was built. On Sundays he's our song leader, his fingers "snapping" out the tempo so Mrs. Stanton can hear and follow (not that it's varied by a metronome beat for decades). Years before, Ethel and Sherwood raised a family up there in the house on the horizon, but the kids all grew up and moved to more promising oil patches out in West Texas, so the Tripps always have a welcome plate for me at their table. The only children in that Sunday room—beside the pastor—are the three Dexter boys, ages eight, six, and four, each one scrubbed cleaner than a dairyman's milk pail and watching me closer than a pitcher eyeing the man on first.

At the appointed moment, Mr. Nichols and I "uncover" Jesus, or at least as much of him as you can symbolize in a cup of juice and a bit of a cracker. Then I raise the cup and the cracker before them all, saying: "Take and eat; this is my body.... Drink, for this is my blood of the covenant...I will never again drink of this fruit of the vine until that day when I drink it new with you in my Father's kingdom" (Matt. 26:26-29).

Finally, in silence, we eat a meal that never was meant to satisfy hunger, but to feed it.

That scene happened sixty years ago. Though I had a part in the Tripps' funerals, I know not where life led for any of the rest within that room. For all of us, even the Dexter boys, life has happened, and death for most. No doubt if I'd spent the balance of my days there, we'd have butted heads and had some forgiving and some apologizing to do. But like an echo I cannot unhear are those words I once read among them, those words about "when I drink it new with you in my Father's kingdom."

Apparently, Jesus thought big thoughts, saw big outcomes, and even imagined that all of us—all of us thick-headed nibblers and sippers—would one day feast with him in his Father's kingdom. He really thought we could all make it, together. He thought that the whole world could be affected by just such improbable people and modest moments such as Communion Sunday at Walker Church. I do hope he is right.

An Anchor and Horizon

When God desired to show even more clearly to the heirs of the promise the unchangeable character of his purpose, he guaranteed it by an oath, so that... we who have taken refuge might be strongly encouraged to seize the hope set before us. We have this hope, a sure and steadfast anchor of the soul, a hope that enters the inner shrine behind the curtain, where Jesus, a forerunner on our behalf, has entered....

(Heb. 6:17-20)

The obituary of Hugo Gryn, one of Great Britain's most respected rabbis, reported one of his childhood memories. Its site was the Nazi concentration camp of Auschwitz where Gryn and his family were imprisoned. Even in that desperate, hopeless place, his father, a devout Orthodox Jew, refused to forego observance of the *shabbat* or Jewish festivals. On one occasion, his father took a piece of string and put it in a bit of butter and lit it to make a *shabbat* candle.

Young Hugo was furious and protested, "Father, that is all the butter we have!"

"Without food we can live for weeks," his father said. "But we cannot live for a minute without hope."[1]

French philosopher Gabriel Marcel would nod in wholehearted agreement. "Hope is for the soul what breathing is for the living organism," he wrote. "Where hope is lacking, the soul dries up and withers."[2]

Another who would concur would be the Austrian psychiatrist, Viktor Frankl, who was imprisoned like the Gryn family at Auschwitz. In Frankl's classic *Man's Search for Meaning*, he tells of one evening in the sixth winter of World War II when prisoners' hopes had fallen to near zero.

The day had begun with the cruel announcement of yet another absurd "crime" now punishable by immediate death by hanging. Midday, a theft of some potatoes from the pantry was discovered, and over the public address system the commandant ordered that the "burglar" must be handed over to him or there would be no food for any of the prisoners for twenty-four hours. So, as evening fell, 2,500 emaciated, starving men, choosing to "fast," returned to their huts without supper or hope of breakfast or lunch tomorrow. Their despair was deepened by the fact that several of their number had died recently, either of sickness or suicide, but really from the loss of hope.

The weight of these deaths, and the unspoken reason for them, hung heavy in the air.

Finally, as the last straw, the light in Frankl's hut went out. The warden of the hut, a fellow prisoner, quickly and wisely spoke into the crucifying darkness; he urged the men not to give way to despair. And, to give them encouragement, he called Frankl's name and asked him to speak to his miserable, now invisible companions buried in that darkened hut.

Frankl says he was in no mood to give any such talk; he too was cold and hungry, irritable and tired. But he made himself talk to the other prisoners—about hope. He urged them, in recalling all they had lost, not to forget what they still had. They still had all their bones intact; they were still alive, and thus there was the possibility that their losses could be restored. And who knew what asset might come to them from all their suffering.

He talked to them of realism, admitting that as a scientifically inclined man, he figured his chances of surviving this ordeal were about one in twenty. "But I also told them that, in spite of this, I had no intention of losing hope and giving up. For no man knew what the future would bring, much less the next hour."

He told them that human life, under any circumstances, never ceases to have a meaning and that they must summon their courage to be sure "that the hopelessness of our struggle did not detract from its dignity and its meaning." "Someone," he added, "looks down on each of us in difficult hours—a friend, a wife, somebody alive or dead, or a God—and he would not expect us to disappoint him. He would hope to find us suffering proudly—not miserably—knowing how to die."

Finally, Frankl spoke to them of their sacrifice. In this-worldly terms the sacrifice of their lives was admittedly pointless. But he said that even if their lives were lost, they could personally dedicate them as a sacrifice that others might not have to die so cruelly. They did not have to die for nothing. They could choose to persevere in hope.

When the darkened hut's electric light finally flared up again, he could see that his words had found their mark. "I saw the miserable figures of my friends limping toward me to thank me with tears in their eyes."[3]

We know of Auschwitz only from reports or memoirs or as after-the-fact tourists, walking its grounds. But from the extremity of the experience of those who faced its horrors, the testimony is carved in granite: We cannot live a minute without hope.

Or, as the New Testament says, hope is a "sure and steadfast anchor of the soul." Without hope we are cast upon an uncaring sea, all compasses worthless, and defenseless against the pounding winds and watery depths. Hope, as a sure and steadfast anchor of the soul, saves us. It gives us something to tie our lives to, something to hold us in place when "all hell breaks loose."

But if our understanding of hope goes no further than this, we will have seen only the half of it. For the same passage that speaks of hope as an anchor also speaks of hope as being "set before us"—as a goal in the distance, a mountain to be climbed. It speaks of hope in mobile images, as entering the inner shrine behind the curtain—a reference to the Holy of Holies within the Jerusalem temple, to the curtained cubicle where the ancient artifacts of Israel's faith were deposited, to the "throne room" of God, a place the Bible elsewhere calls a place of "thick darkness" (1 Kgs. 8:12, 2 Chron. 6:1, Ps. 97:2, et al).

So, hope is more than a source of anchorage and strength against the storm, something we can by faith clasp in the hour of need. Hope is also a great good that eludes us, a goal that is not yet in our possession. It is a vision, a horizon "before us," calling and tugging us deeper into life and into the frightening yet fascinating mystery.

The Latin-writing theologians of yesteryear even coined an expression to speak of this future orientation: *status viatoris*. In their construal of it, to be a *viator* was to be "one on the way" and *status viatoris* was therefore the condition or state of being on the way. This was the opposite of *status comprehensoris*, the condition or state of having already arrived or comprehended (see Phil. 3:13). In one sense, from the moment of birth we are all *status viatoris*, persons in transition and movement, on the way through life. But when hope's full dimensions are understood, this status accrues a deeper significance and higher goal.

When hope moves from being just an anchor to become a vision also, then *status comprehensoris* is abandoned and *status viatoris* begins in earnest. We move from being creatures progressing through life—and vainly imagining we "have our act together"—to understanding ourselves as persons anchored in eternity and also called to something profound, elusive, and loftier. We become pilgrims looking for a better, higher plain—and not just for ourselves! Hope calls us to become all we can become,[4] to be what God can make of us, to dream the dreams of God and to seek "thy kingdom come, thy will be done on earth." Hope, as it did for Abraham, sets us on a journey—if not in search of a promised land, then in search of a world within ourselves and a world outside of us that is more user-friendly than the ugly shock-and-awe debacle now on display. It creates a holy discontent, an unwillingness to settle for the existing.

And since I have delved into Latin, it is fitting here to recall a famous line about hope from the pen of St. Augustine (who wrote more books in Latin than many of us will ever read in English!). He wrote that "Hope has two beautiful daughters whose names are Anger and Courage. Anger at the way things are, and courage to see that they do not remain the same."[5] Hope, as even Augustine understood it, puts us on the road as agents of change, converting us from *comprehensors* to *viators*.

Hope leads us to be persons activated by anger, for example, against the anti-Semitism and racism that ever made an Auschwitz possible and makes the necessity of a twenty-first century Black Lives Matter movement so tragic. And hope leads us to be persons empowered by hope's courage to see that our children not be asked to shoulder burdens we let fall. "Hopeful people are always critical of the present but only because they hold such a bright view of the future. For like nothing else in the world, hope arouses a passion for the possible."[6]

Again I say, we cannot live for a minute without hope—not without the hope that is the soul's anchor in a stormy world, nor the hope that stirs up "good trouble" by disturbing the peace of a world that pretends all is calm and all is bright. To shrink back from the *viator's* calling is to clutch a perverse and selfish brand of hope, hardly reminiscent of "the pioneer and perfecter of our faith, who for the sake of the joy that was before him endured the cross, disregarding its shame, and has taken his seat at the right hand of the throne of God" (Heb. 12:2).

We need not be under any delusion that we are going to right every wrong or remake the whole creation into an Eden of righteousness. But neither are we free from any responsibility to try. To bind up earth's wounds and bury its weapons is our work as surely as it is God's; else, God would not have awakened our hopes by showing us that horizon of a new world. And through our actions, the hopes of others are awakened to seek this world of God's promise. How we shall overcome, and where the path may wind before God's vision becomes our reality, I cannot guess. But I do believe that "anyone who wants to reach the new world across the sea will start off for the port of departure on his own feet and with the means of transport at his disposal in this old world, even though he realizes that very different forces will be needed before he can land in the new world and become its citizen."[7]

NOTES

[1]Thomas G. Long, *Preaching from Memory to Hope* (Louisville, KY: Westminster John Knox), 132.

[2]Gabriel Marcel, *Homo Viator: Introduction to a Metaphysics of Hope*, trans. Emma Crauford (New York: Harper & Row, 1962), 11. John R. Claypool, *The Hopeful Heart* (Harrisburg, PA: Morehouse Publishing, 2003), 3, restates Marcel: "What breath is to the physical body, hope is to the human spirit."

[3]Viktor E. Frankl, *Man's Search for Meaning* (Boston: Beacon Press, 2006), 80-84.

[4]In the earliest of Dag Hammarskjold's "markings" was his hope at twenty years of age to become "a man who had become what he could, and was what he was." *Markings*, trans. Leif Sjoberg and W.H. Auden (New York: Alfred A. Knopf, 1998), 6.

[5]"This expression is widely cited but seems to have come to us via Anselm of Canterbury, who attributes it to Augustine." Allan Boesak, *Dare We Speak of Hope?* (Grand Rapids: Wm. B. Eerdmans Publishing Co., 2014), 43, fn. 1.

[6]William Sloane Coffin, *A Passion for the Possible* (Louisville, KY: Westminster John Knox, 1993), 3.

[7]Wolff, *Anthropology of the Old Testament* (Philadelphia: Fortress Press, 1974), 155.

The Future of Hope

Will God not grant justice to his chosen ones who cry to him day and night? Will he delay long in helping them? I tell you, he will quickly grant justice to them. And yet, when the Son of Man comes, will he find faith on earth?
(Luke 18:8b)

Twenty years ago an international group of Christian theologians met twice for lengthy discussions concerning "The Future of Hope." They gathered in response to a shared perception that in the preceding three decades "a major cultural shift had taken place in the attitudes of Western culture about the future." Instead of the resolute optimism that had long dominated the Western mind, they observed the emergence of what they called "a culture of ambiguity."

Assumptions and certainties that had anchored previous generations were being gobbled up by data that could not be winked away. As a consequence, in Western minds, the future now was "ambiguous." As Christian theologians, their concern was that in this strategic hour the biblical understanding of hope was making "less and less claim" on the populace "because it is ignored, forgotten, or rejected, or manipulated and marketed by its proponents."[1] Hope, in their assessment, whether in secular or Christian dress, was on the ropes.

The ensuing decades have only corroborated their reading. As just one indication of America's "culture of ambiguity," one might note that in four of the five presidential elections in this period the themes of hope (Obama, Biden) and/or nostalgia (Trump) were dominant. One indication of the lessening of the biblical tradition of hope might be the steady exodus of Americans—most noticeably among younger adults—from churches, as numerous polls across the past quarter of a century have documented.

The Israeli scholar Yuval Noah Harari has been among those tracking global trends during these years and in *21 Lessons for the 21*st *Century* he offers his assessment of the daunting predicaments we now face. Though Harari says he still manages "to wake up cheerful in the morning,"[2] he believes that as a society we are currently "in the nihilist moment of disillusionment and anger" about our loss of assumptions and expectations. He offers this advice:

The first step is to tone down the prophecies of doom and switch from panic mode to bewilderment. Panic is a form of hubris. It comes from the smug feeling that one knows exactly where the world is heading: down. Bewilderment is more humble and therefore more clearsighted. Do you feel like running down the street crying "The apocalypse is upon us"? Try telling yourself, "No, it's not that. Truth is, I just don't understand what's going on in the world."[3]

The truth is, we have created a world we no longer understand or feel we can control. Ours is a time of bewilderment and reflecting a "culture of ambiguity" in which old certainties no longer speak convincingly while new ones are not yet clear. To date, anger and nostalgia have been our most notable responses. Hope, in forms other than political nostrums, has been having more difficulty getting on stage.

This is especially so for the Christian tradition of hope, as the theologians' conferences in 2000–2001 presaged. Most crucially, today's heightened awareness of continuing racial, economic, and gender injustices has raised the question of why, if there is anything to Christianity's gospel of the kingdom of God on earth, why aren't there more evidences of it after all these centuries? Just how much suffering will God permit before we see the righting of wrong and the age of peace begun?

The problem is as ancient as the New Testament, of course. Luke's gospel exposes his own generation's struggle to persist in hope by means of a parable (18:1-8) that Luke introduces by saying it is "about [our] need to pray always and not to lose heart." The parable is about a woman who is being abused by some "opponent," and so she seeks relief through the courts. Unfortunately, her complaint is assigned to a judge who "neither feared God nor had respect for people." Nonetheless, the lady persists, finding endless ways to pester this judge until finally, wearied by her, the judge rules in her favor.

As the story goes, Jesus then points to God as the polar opposite of this heartless judge, and then he asks two rhetorical questions. First, won't God grant justice to the downtrodden? And second, will God be slow in redressing their oppression? And, if you are slow to give the expected response, Jesus boldly answers for you: "I tell you, [God] will quickly grant justice to them."

If that word "quickly" weren't in the story, this parable would likely never have been reported. But by putting a timer of God's delivery of justice, the story not only becomes memorable but it also places hope in jeopardy. The word "quickly" and a delay of two thousand years are difficult to reconcile. But to crown the awkwardness of the entire scene, the parable concludes with yet another question from Jesus: "And yet, when the Son of Man comes, will he find faith on earth?"

Maintaining a belief in a God who cares and who grants justice to the downtrodden has never been easy. Jesus seems to say as much in his uncharacteristic questioning about faith's future. So, the problem of our hope's credibility has lain at the heart of Christian faith from its inception.

Unfortunately, I have no solutions to offer as the magic answer, nor theological sleight-of-hand maneuvers to dazzle you—not even a clever word-play to disguise the open wound. The problem of continuing suffering in a world God supposedly loves remains a heartbreaking mystery and faith's greatest intellectual challenge. The best I have to offer in response is another question and then three suggestions.

LORD, *to whom shall we go?* This is my question even as it was Simon Peter's question long ago when defections from Jesus' company were numerous, when "many...turned back and no longer went about with him" (John 6:66-69). When Jesus saw them leaving, he asked the Twelve if they also wished to depart. But Simon replied: "LORD, to whom shall we go?"

This question leaps across centuries and confronts me with assessing alternatives to the Christian faith. Do I know of another faith or philosophy that does a better job of "answering" the problem of innocent suffering? Of life's enigmas, inequities, and tensions? I ask this in sincerity. For if there is a better faith, a better "savior" to be followed, then I ought not rest in Christianity's half-truths just because they are familiar and culturally accepted.

Peter, knowing no viable alternatives, answered Jesus with a profession: "You have the words of eternal life. We have come to believe and know that you are the Holy One of God." That was one man's long-ago answer. But each of us must do our own deciding. So, for me, it comes down to this: Does the fact that Christian faith rests upon a death and a resurrection, upon suffering endured and overcome, upon God's entering into and sharing this agony with us—does this hold sufficient gravity that I can credit it as being the most promising faith-story available? If you can, and I hope you can join me in this choice, here are three suggestions as to how to keep this faith alive in hope and love:

Become a slow reader.

I am referring to the reading of the Bible, which was written so that through its "encouragement we might have hope" (Rom. 15:4). My point is that "if there is a secret to getting involved with God through the pages of scripture, then perhaps it is this: *turn the pages slowly.*"[4] One of the students in Ellen Davis' introductory Old Testament course at Duke Divinity School once told her that when she had begun the course she thought her problem would be that she read too slowly and wouldn't be able to keep up. But midway through the course she came to see that her problem was that she read too fast. All her undergraduate classes and secular work experience had taught her to prize the ability to work through vast amounts of print quickly. But, as Davis says, "the Bible discourages us from making mileage a measure of success." Davis continues:

> In many cases, [the Bible's] riches are perceptible only to those who move slowly, like mushroom hunters, peering closely where at first there appears to be nothing at all to see. Almost always it is useful to linger over a word or a phrase that seems strangely chosen... For it is by means of words that the Bible performs its revelatory function. An unexpected word can jar us into contemplating new possibilities about how things really are. An ambiguous word jogs our minds onto a completely different track. Often when reading one portion of scripture, we run across words that echo another passage. Thus the biblical writers lead us subtly to make connections—between events in the text and likewise between events in our lives—that we had never previously imagined.[5]

Please do not overlook three phrases within this statement: "jar us into... new possibilities," "jog our minds onto a completely different track," and "make connections...never previously imagined." Each of these is pointing to the gift of hope. And each of these shouts once again that unhurried, careful attention to the promise/word is the ignition point of hope. If we are to keep hope alive, we must ponder our texts reverently, thoughtfully, inquisitively. Like a lozenge placed in one's mouth to dissolve solely, so is the word to be savored and experienced as a stimulant to hope.

Talk less.

In this suggestion I am referring specifically to prayer (although some of us might profitably use the counsel for many more circumstances of life). And I am attempting to honor Luke's note that Jesus' parable is about the imperative of prayer if we are not to lose heart. In one sense, it seems needless to say that prayer has a crucial role to play in hope's livelihood. How might we imagine that a robust hope in God could ever be maintained apart from frequent contact with the God of hope? I am, however, suggesting a kind of praying that is atypical, a kind of praying that is less consumed with storming heaven's gates with today's list of grievances, and more given to the discipline of silence in God's presence.

Unquestionably, there is a place for talking in our prayers, and there is a healthiness to voicing our sorrows and fears and yearnings before God—what Stanley Grenz winsomely called "cries for the kingdom."[6] But I also recall that Jesus had nothing good to say about "long" prayers and that the one model prayer he gave can be uttered in less than thirty seconds. Even so, the scriptures also tell us Jesus engaged in long periods of prayer. The only satisfying explanation of this for me is that for Jesus, prayer was more a matter of listening than of talking. It was a conscious seeking of God's voice of guidance, not an extended rehearsing of information already known to God about the need for this guidance. It was a quieting of the mind and heart before God that the immensity of God might swallow up the fright of any given moment. "Be still and know that I am God."

Most certainly this manner of prayer may be likened to the meditation upon the promise/word I have talked about so often in these pages. Into the silent waiting of a scripture-formed mind, illumination comes, imagination springs to life, and hope stirs. In other words, hope comes from beyond us; it arises from the quietness of trust.

In the prayer passages of the Bible we often see the word "heart," a word we associate with our affections or moods. Students of the Hebrew language have shown, however, that in many cases when "heart" appears in our English translations, it would be better translated as "imagination."[7] If this be so, it sheds a new understanding upon the classic liturgical invitation to worship and prayer: "Lift up your hearts!" The call is a summons to lift up our imagination to the Holy One, to offer to God our ability to perceive a "new thing," to let God jog our anxious minds onto a completely different track. "Lift up your hearts" is, then, a plea to hush our anxious jabbering and allow the Eternal to grant the vision glorious. If we are to keep hope alive, we must talk less and listen more.

Cherish community.

Hope's audacity is too great to carry alone for long. It lives best within the "nibble and sip" fellowship I've written about earlier. I might even say it stays alive *only* within that fellowship, where there is the encouragement of other "fools" who harbor this preposterously absurd idea that God is alive and making all things new.

Our Christian ancestors soon sensed this and even wrote about it. One of them, after urging believers to "hold fast to our hope, without wavering, for he who promised is faithful," added a practical how-to: "And…consider how to provoke one another to love and good deeds, not neglecting to meet together, as is the habit of some, but encouraging one another, and all the more as you see the day approaching" (Heb. 10:23-25).

Here within the community at worship is where we hear the voice of others testifying in word and song to realities that only hope can see. Here we "lift up our imagination" in expectancy to the giver of all good and perfect gifts. Here the treasure book of promise is opened and its words are reverently read and interpreted. And here, through bread and wine, we rehearse and receive a foretaste of the feast that is to come. Here is where hope finds a welcoming home.

This community will surely assume new shapes in days to come, but the hoping community of Christ will not perish from the earth. "Until he comes," its daily manna will be the word and the spirit; the promise and the silent waiting. For the present this community, like everything else in creation, feels somewhat bewildered. Hope is a challenge. But like Israel in exile, there is for us also a grand promise: "I am about to do a new thing; now it springs forth, do you not perceive it? I will make a way in the wilderness, and rivers in the desert" (Isa. 43:19).

NOTES

[1] *The Future of Hope: Christian Tradition Amid Modernity and Postmodernity*, eds. Miroslav Volf and William Katerberg (Grand Rapids: Wm. B. Eerdmans Publishing Co. Publishing, 2004), ix-x.

[2] Yuval Noah Harari, *21 Lessons for the 21st Century* (New York: Spiegel & Grau, 2019), 319.
[3] Ibid., 18.

[4] Ellen Davis, *Getting Involved with God: Rediscovering the Old Testament* (Cambridge, MA: Cowley Publications, 2001), 3.

[5] Ibid.

[6] Stanley J. Grenz, *Prayer: The Cry for the Kingdom* (Peabody, MA: Hendrickson Publishing, 1988).

[7] *The Art of Reading Scripture*, eds. Ellen F. Davis and Richard B. Hays (Grand Rapids: Wm. B. Eerdmans Publishing Co. Publishing, 2003), 11.

PART 3

Facing the End with Lively Hope

If for this life only we have hoped in Christ,
we are of all people most to be pitied.
But in fact Christ has been raised from the dead,
the first fruits of those who have died.
(1 Cor. 15:19-20 NIV)

Lead gently, LORD, and slow,
For oh, my steps are weak,
And ever as I go,
Some soothing silence speak;

That I may turn my face
Through doubt's obscurity
Toward thine abiding-place,
E'en tho' I cannot see.

For lo, the way is dark;
Through mist and cloud I grope,
Save for that fitful spark,
The little flame of hope.

Lead gently, LORD, and slow,
For fear that I may fall;
I know not where to go
Unless I hear thy call.

My fainting soul doth yearn
For thy green hills afar;
So let thy mercy burn—
My greater, guiding star!

—Paul Laurence Dunbar (1872–1906)

Left Behind vs. Hope on Planet Earth

Listen, I will tell you a mystery! We will not all die, but we will all be changed, in a moment, in the twinkling of an eye, at the last trumpet. For the trumpet will sound, and the dead will be raised imperishable, and we will be changed.
(1 Cor. 15:51-52)

"Even so, come quickly, Lord Jesus!" You're not likely to hear this petition offered next Sunday in church. If you do, you may be sure some heads will snap up, checking to see who just prayed it. Oddly, this now-startling prayer was one of the most frequent and ardent prayers of the earliest church. Jesus' return was their great hope.

Today, however, the idea of the return of Jesus is either the source of jokes or an ignored thicket of irrelevancies or an esoteric obsession. My impression, overall, is that the second coming of Jesus is perceived, even by churchgoers, mostly as a spooky threat hovering over us. How did a hope that was so central to our ancestors become such a kill-joy nightmare for so many people today?

There are many reasons, but two are easily named. The first is the error of giving literal value to symbolic biblical language. If you read the Revelation to John or even the Gospels of Matthew, Mark, or Luke you will come upon entire chapters that have to do with "last days," or eschatological matters. These chapters (Matthew 24, Mark 13, Luke 21) can make your blood run cold *if* you give literal significance to everything within them. However, they—and other such passages—were never meant to be interpreted literally.

These passages use apocalyptic language (more about this in "Abandon Hope"), which even in that day was understood to be raw, graphic, and exaggerated speech—not the careful, measured speech of data. Thomas G. Long puts it this way: "The eschatological and apocalyptic language of the Bible is not about predicting the future; it is primarily a way of seeing the present in the light of hope."[1] It was meant to stir imagination, not to give information.

But when interpreters of scripture ignore this basic linguistic fact and then identify certain current events that supposedly match selected verses about Jesus' return, we have a first-class mess on our hands. And this is a second reason why we now find the return of Jesus to be a source of confusion and fear rather than hope. For some authors have done precisely this, and their interpretations have been so successfully packaged and sold to the masses that their views are now believed to be the gospel truth about the return of Jesus.

The two best-known examples of this practice are the best-selling book of the 1970s, *The Late Great Planet Earth,* and the sixteen novels and two commercial movies of the *Left Behind* series (1995–2007). For hope's sake, we need to give them a second and more critical look.

The originating author behind the *Left Behind* phenomenon was the conservative Christian pastor and right-wing political activist, Tim LaHaye. Writer Jerry Jenkins artfully converted LaHaye's ideas into the experience of one twentieth-century family in a series of novels filled with demonic conspiracies, cyberspace technology, romance, and military moxie.

The series begins with Captain Rayford Steele, the pilot of a 747 flight to London, encountering midflight the loss of the majority of his passengers. One second they are snugly belted into their seats, but in the next second they are nowhere to be found. They have vanished! Radio communications with other airliners confirm the same is happening everywhere. Without trace or warning, millions of people throughout the world have vanished. When Steele returns to his state-side home, he discovers both his son and wife are among the missing.

In this manner Rayford Steele and the readers of the *Left Behind* books are introduced to a key concept of LaHaye's second coming schema, the Rapture, the instantaneous snatching up of all Christians from the earth. In the following books, Captain Steele, now born-again, attempts to thwart the world-dominating Antichrist during a vicious seven-year, post-Rapture period that LaHaye and his predecessors call the Great Tribulation.

More than fifty million copies of these books have been sold, and a surprising amount of American environmental and Mideast policy has been influenced by the end-times narrative spun in them.[2]

But before there was *Left Behind,* there was its 1970s predecessor, *The Late Great Planet Earth.* Though it had none of the story-centered appeal of *Left Behind,* Hal Lindsey's single, slender paperback sold more than six million copies in less than six years. Using the same understanding of Christ's return as LaHaye and Jenkins, Lindsey claimed that the Cold War politics and cultural shifts of his day were fulfillments of prophecy and clear signs that earth's end was near. Lindsey's book, too, had impact upon American politics and policy.[3]

The schema that these two products popularized so successfully—its theological name is *premillennial dispensationalism*—is the latest, but certainly not the only last-times schema developed across the past two thousand years by faithful Christians. Some are as unadorned as saying Christ's return refers simply to his "return" to receive dying Christians. Others, such as premillennial dispensationalism, are more complex.[4] However, no common agreement has ever been reached among all these schemas, and this is likely because, as conservative New Testament scholar F.F. Bruce believed: "Holy Writ does not provide us with the means of plotting the course of future events."[5] N.T. Wright picturesquely adds that "all Christian language about the future is a set of signposts pointing into a mist."[6] Nonetheless, millions have accepted the ideas of Lindsey and LaHaye as being the only and final word on the subject.

I believe premillennial dispensationalism (which I will hereafter refer to as PD) is the major current culprit in converting the grand promise of the return of Christ into a fearful spectacle. In the name of Christian hope, PD ironically presents a vision of the future that stifles hope. The Bible's ultimate promise, that this world will be set to rights and the goodness seen in Jesus will reign on earth—this grand hope and goal—is lost in PD's vision of horrifying events and bloody battles. Just two features of its schema demonstrate this unfortunate twist.

The first of these I call the "domino flaw." PD begins with the conviction that history is like a ticking clock, with each hour bringing us closer to the final hour. The schema continues by claiming that we can discern how to read this clock correctly by examining certain verses in the Old Testament book of Daniel. With Daniel's decoding information deciphered, as PD claims it does, we are able to identify a sequential list of historic events that lead to the Second Coming. For instance, a primary event in this countdown to the "last days" was the establishment of Israel as a political state in 1948. Other events such as the establishment of the United Nations in 1945, or September 11, 2001, or certain Mideastern conflicts may be crucial indicators of where we are in the run-up to Armageddon—depending on which PD teacher you listen to, and when.

There is, therefore, a divinely predetermined series of historical events set up like dominoes, each one bringing us nearer to the End. Moreover, these dominoes are mostly horrid events, precursors of even greater calamities to follow. But because they are divinely appointed, there is nothing humans can do to change the script. Floods, earthquakes, plagues, famines, and wars are the inescapable future of the planet—and therefore efforts to avoid ecological disasters or broker peace treaties are ultimately pointless. Our mandate as stewards of creation is nullified, and earth's future is an unalterable series of horrific implosions ending in a blood bath of galling proportions (Armageddon).

Never mind that even in the Revelation, which PD purports to interpret, the only weapon that Jesus wields is the two-edged sword of his word (Rev. 1:16, 19:15; Eph. 6:17). Never mind that this schema tacitly admits that Jesus' ethic of non-violence is ultimately ineffective. After all is said and done, the fist of might decides the right. Or, as one summarized it: "For God so loved the world that he sent World War III."

A second hope-stealing facet of PD is its central feature of the Rapture, that is, the snatching up of all earth's Christians into the clouds while a seven-year period of unparalleled horror is loosed on earth by the reigning Antichrist. No other schema of the "last days" includes the idea of a Rapture; this remains PD's unique contribution to the discussion. But within PD's lined-up dominoes, a "rapture" is needed to make the sequence unfold as it should.

There are problems, though, not the least of which is the questionable extraterrestrial interpretation PD gives to the one New Testament passage that even suggests a Rapture: "For the LORD himself, with a cry of command, with the archangel's call and with the sound of God's trumpet, will descend from heaven, and the dead in Christ will rise first. Then we who are alive, who are left, will be caught up in the clouds together with them to meet the LORD in the air: and so we will be with the LORD forever" (1 Thess. 4:16-17).

Were this the only time Paul wrote of the experience of believers at the time of the return of Christ, PD's Rapture might have more merit. But, in fact, Paul spoke of this moment two other times. In 1 Corinthians 15:23-27, 51-54 Paul says those who are living when Christ returns will be "changed" or "transformed"—not be "caught up in the air" as in 1 Thessalonians. And in Philippians 3:20-21, in a discussion of the Philippians' citizenship being in heaven although they are residents of an earthly Roman colony, Paul says those who are alive when Christ returns will experience a transformation of their bodies so as to be conformed to Jesus' body. Again, there is nothing said about a Rapture occurring.

All three of these passages must be viewed together before determining what is meant by any one of them. Attempting to do that, many scholars believe the Thessalonian passage reflects the Philippian context of a Roman emperor coming to a colony of his empire. In this situation, the citizens of the colony would go out to greet the emperor at some distance from the city; to remain within the city walls would be disrespectful. It would appear as though they didn't care to welcome him properly. But upon going out to greet him, they would not loiter there, but would escort him regally back into the city. Thus, as N.T. Wright says:

When Paul speaks of "meeting" the LORD "in the air," the point is precisely not—as in the popular rapture theology—that the saved believers would then stay up in the air somewhere, away from earth. The point is that, having gone out to meet their returning LORD, they will escort him royally into his domain, that is, back to the place they have come from. Even when we realize that this is highly charged metaphor, not literal description, the meaning is the same as in the parallel in Philippians 3:20: "Our citizenship is in heaven, and it is from there that we are expecting a Savior, the LORD Jesus Christ."[7]

The promise of the return of Christ was not given as a threat, but as a joyful affirmation of who holds the upper hand in the human, earthly story. It was given to encourage us to persevere in our assigned tasks until the Master comes (Matt. 24:46). When PD twists this promise so that human compassion and industry are pointless, distorts it so that our role as caretakers is trumped by God's planned destruction of it, perverts it so that the end contradicts everything Jesus lived and died for, and then expects us to rejoice in earth's agonies because each bad news report actually brings us closer to God's triumph—this is a gutting of the very hope that God embedded within creation, enfleshed in Jesus, and promised to the followers of the Lamb.

John Henry Cardinal Newman (1801–1890) lived during the days that PD was being formulated by British students of the Bible. Newman, however, offered a very different understanding of history and of the human future. He agreed with the originators of PD about the linear concept of history, that it was headed to a future ending. But he disagreed about where that end-point should be imagined.

In light of the New Testament witness, Newman said the End that most profoundly mattered happened at Calvary and Easter. Holy Week was the great event toward which all history was tending. We must, therefore, think of history not as continuing to run toward some future date but as running along the End, as on the brink of it, and every moment is now lived on the rim, on the edge of time, and every day alive not with foreboding but with opportunity and responsibility. "Christ, then, is ever at our doors; as near [two thousand years ago] as now, and not nearer now than then, and not nearer when he comes than now."[8] In this matter, my vote goes to Cardinal Newman, not to Lindsey and LaHaye.

When we speak of the return of Christ, then, we are not talking about rejoicing while a heartbreaking series of second-coming catastrophes brings us ever nearer to the End. Nor are we talking about being "snatched up" from this world for a seven-year siesta in cloudland while the world below convulses. No, we are talking about the grand fruition of God's long march to a creation now full-purposed. We are talking about the universe's deep and reconciling alleluia to its loving Creator and Sustainer. We are talking about this world finally saying "thank you" to the One who would not let go. And we are talking about our assurance that the future is secure in the hands of our crucified and exalted LORD.

The second coming of Christ means we have not seen the last of this Nazarene. For "when earth's last picture is painted and the tubes are twisted and dried"[9] we will see him again, this man of truth and grace at the center of God's heart. Simply, profoundly, and stubbornly, the second coming of Jesus says just one beautiful thing: in the end…God!

NOTES

[1]Thomas G. Long, *Preaching from Memory to Hope* (Louisville, KY: Westminster John Knox, 2009), 129.

[2]America's unwavering support of Israel, in spite of its disregard of Palestinian peoples and claims, and the recognition of Jerusalem as Israel's capital may be noted. Also, American departure from the Paris Accords and denial of climate science are influenced by the assumptions and teaching of this schema.

[3]See Barbara Rossing, *The Rapture Exposed: The Message of Hope in the Book of Revelation* (New York: Basic Books, 2004) for a discussion of the political and policy effects.

[4]See James Robert Ross, "Evangelical Alternatives," in *Handbook of Biblical Prophecy*, Carl Armerding and W. Ward Gasque, eds. (Grand Rapids: Baker Book House, 1977), 117-129; Timothy P. Weber, "Dispensationalism," in *A New Handbook of Christian Theology*, Donald Musser and Joseph Price, eds. (Nashville: Abingdon Press, 1992), 125-127; Dale C. Allison Jr., "Eschatology of the NT," in *The New Interpreter's Dictionary of the Bible* D–H, vol. 2, Katherine Doob Sakenfeld, ed. (Nashville: Abingdon Press, 2007), 294-299; and Debra J. Mumford, *Envisioning the Reign of God: Preaching for Tomorrow* (Valley Forge, PA: Judson Press, 2019).

[5]F.F. Bruce, "Foreword," in *Handbook of Biblical Prophecy*, 7.

[6]N.T. Wright, *Surprised by Hope: Rethinking Heaven, the Resurrection, and the Mission of the Church* (New York: HarperOne, 2008), 132.

[7]Ibid. 133.

[8]Cited in *Handbook of Biblical Prophecy*, 9.

[9]Rudyard Kipling, "L'Envoi" to *The Seven Seas*, 1896.

Resurrection: Where Hope Breaks Free[1]

When they looked up, they saw that the stone, which was very large, had already been rolled back. As they entered the tomb, they saw a young man, dressed in a robe, sitting on the right side; and they were alarmed. But he said to them, "Do not be alarmed; you are looking for Jesus of Nazareth, who was crucified. He has been raised; he is not here."
(Mark 16:4-7)

The most astonishing act of God within the Gospels is the resurrection of Jesus from the dead. Sunday's first light revealed that Friday's crucifixion might have been a hollow victory for the powers that be. Women visit Jesus' borrowed tomb at dawn and are told "He is not here." Upon their report, disciples run, investigate, and return, verifying the report. Emotions already ravaged by the weekend are overwhelmed by yet more questions. Someone says Mary Magdalene has actually seen and even talked to him! Really? A trickle of rumors grows that Pilate's atrocity has been vetoed, that God really has raised Jesus from the grave. But can that be true? In half-belief, various disciples begin to whisper a question to one another: "He is risen?" In the dizziness of the next days, their questioning whisper becomes a stout declaration as one after another astonished eyewitness insists: "He *is* risen! He is risen, indeed!"

Those Easter words are now almost cliché worship words for many of us. We typically hear them as part of Easter morning services and sermons assuring us that there is life beyond death. But much more is involved in the resurrection of Jesus than evidence of life beyond death. The larger truth is that human history itself turns a page with the resurrection of Jesus. The silent Saturday world ruled by death and defeat is left behind on that Sunday when hope breaks free. Friday's crucified rabbi is shown to be the one who begins the end, for in him the promised tomorrow is unfurled and the era of God's reign is begun.

The idea of a life beyond death was widespread in Jesus' day. Many Jews believed in such. Within that belief, however, was their assumption that this resurrection to life would occur on the "last day" as one of the final "end time" events. When "the day" came, the dead would be raised to life and the long-yearned-for kingdom of God would appear in life-restoring power. But again, this was to be a resurrection of *all* the dead, not just one man.

But when just one man, Jesus, who had ceaselessly proclaimed the arrival of the promised kingdom, when this one man returned to his followers as alive from a hideous death, the conclusion was that God's promised tomorrow had already begun![2] The vice-grip of the powers of sin and death had been broken. The "end time" was already here.

So out of the impenetrable darkness of death the light of hope emerged, a hope not only for life after death but also for a world in which God was dramatically at work for life's sake—a world no longer imprisoned by the consequences of the past and fearful of the future, but a world freed to become all God had dreamed for it to be. That open tomb opened a new era of history for all creation.

The magnitude of this claim may not be grasped until we place it up against a popular alternate interpretation of the Resurrection. Let a story from my past illumine the contrast.

Some years ago I found myself at a very low place. The stress I felt was almost unbearable, and such hope as sustained me was being sucked from me week by week. Deep within me was the desire to press on—if only to save face—but I honestly did not think anything I could do or say was going to make any difference. Every day was a journey through desolate territory.

One afternoon, while in the darkness of that depressing valley, I drove past a public garden and, not even knowing why, I pulled into the parking lot and began walking around the place. Eventually I found myself standing in a deeply shaded nook of the garden, staring at one of its many botanical information signs.

Across the top of the sign was the word SUCCESSION. The first sentence on the sign told me that this was the term used to describe "the natural progression of change that occurs over time in an ecosystem." It went on to tell of the changes brought to ecosystems by storms, wind, drought, insects, diseases, and such. Finally, it mentioned fire and noted that "what was a towering forest one day could be a pile of smoldering ashes the next." That sign now had all my attention, for that is how I felt—a burned-out specimen amid a once-mighty forest, but now just a smoldering ash heap.

The sign's next sentence came like a lightning bolt: "What appears to be a lifeless landscape is simply an ecosystem on the verge of succession." My eyes glued onto the words "lifeless landscape...on the verge of succession" and then pushed on to read the reminder that in 1980 Mount Saint Helens, in the Pacific Northwest, had experienced a volcanic eruption that leveled pristine forests and covered all their vegetation and wildlife in a thick layer of ash. But two years later, a lone lupine tree grew in the ash, and year by year grasses and wildflowers and small trees began to cover those slopes once again. "A lifeless landscape…on the verge of succession."

So it was that a sign "preached" to me the message that the deadness I felt and saw was not all there was; the ecosystem of life would bloom yet again! Here was a heartening, fresh way of picturing my situation, a way that challenged my despair with encouragement and renewed my will to persevere.

In some persons' understanding, what I wandered into that day was the truth of resurrection. For them, resurrection is the assurance that life always overrules death; that even within the ashes there are seeds that will burst into life; that fallen leaves provide the nutrients and soil for tomorrow's growth; that nothing really and finally dies, but simply becomes another continuing life form. To them, resurrection is what the naturalist calls succession. And, as I have related, the emotional boost that came from this way of perceiving my plight brought comfort to me and invited my patience.

But is this what the New Testament means by resurrection? I don't think so. I think the resurrection of Jesus speaks of something far more astounding than the wonder of succession. Resurrection is more than just a redescription of death, a "sacred sample" of the process of nature working itself out. If the Resurrection is anything, it is not natural! It is stupendously unnatural. It is unlike anything else we know about—it is that "something new under the sun" that Ecclesiastes says cannot be found. Resurrection is confoundingly new and different. It is a second act of creation, and it is just as dumbfounding and impenetrable as the first. It is Genesis 1 revisited, only this time it is the re-creation of life out of stark, total death. Jesus was "crucified, *dead*, and buried" says the Apostles' Creed, meaning precisely what it says.

In Jesus' death the whole tragic story of humankind is put to death. When he cried, "It is finished!" that is part of the meaning. As he faced the cross, Jesus said: "Now is the judgment of this world, now the ruler of this world will be driven out" (John 12:31). At Golgotha, divine judgment and the sentence of death were both enacted. The world's bondage to sin comes to an end—full stop—when the Lord of all dies for it and it dies in him. Thus, when God raises Jesus from the dead, all is begun again in fact and in anticipation. A new creation came to be in him! The prison doors of the past swing open to the march of God through human history, outward toward the full and final realization of God's dream for the whole creation.

The full extent of what is being said here cannot be grasped unless we consider the power that death exerts over us. The Resurrection speaks directly to this and is meant to "free those who all their lives were held in slavery by the fear of death" (Heb. 2:15). Tyrants, political bullies, and thugs have long exploited this fear of death, threatening to kill if their way was hindered. But if death has been defeated by Christ's resurrection, the intimidation of bullies loses its ultimacy.[3] The Easter gospel therefore contains political and cultural gravity! El Salvadoran Archbishop Oscar Romero's 1970s unrelenting denunciation of governmental oppression of the poor led to his murder as he celebrated the Mass—and the backbone of his courage was his resurrection faith. Resurrection faith was the heart of Martin Luther King Jr.'s defiant words on the eve of his assassination: "I'm not fearing any man...for mine eyes have seen the glory!"[4]

If all we make of the resurrection of Jesus is a demonstration or proof of life after death or some form of naturalistic immortality, we are shrinking its significance to a sorry pittance of its majesty. These reductions of meaning come from our individualistic insistence that the gospel be about "me" and, in this case, the prolongation of my life eternally. Most certainly, our LORD's resurrection does wondrously assure us of our own resurrection, but more than that, it assures us that all history and creation are headed somewhere good because our God is making all things new. And the grand news is that we are included within the "all things" of God's recreating power.

When our personal story is one of ashes and despair, the encouragement of succession is unquestionably one source of God-given aid. But the grander story, the gospel, is that God, through the resurrection, has once for all lifted the whole creation from death to life and is carrying it to God's own good ends.

There are verses in the Bible and there are theories aplenty concerning what happens when we die, and what becomes of us, and what we shall be like in that promised future life[5]—but they provide little for me other than momentary flirtations with the unknowable. I find no explanation that satisfies my curiosity, and, since we humans don't have an impressive track record of anticipating God's next moves, I prefer to leave all of this in God's hands. My hope is based upon the promise that "all will be made alive in Christ" (1 Cor. 15: 22)—without craving specifics. Concerning what happens when our last breath is exhaled, my mind and heart can agree only on this: Those who die in Christ are alive in the mystery of the Resurrection. It is enough for me in this life and the next to be in the care and keeping of the One who raised Jesus from the dead.

The grandeur of the Resurrection is underlined in my mind by two attending events: Jesus' descent into hell and his ascension. Though the descent is mentioned only once in the New Testament (1 Pet. 3:18-19), this one obscure reference has become well-known by the Apostles' Creed phrase: "he descended into hell." In marked contrast, Jesus' post-resurrection ascension (and heavenly enthronement) is often alluded to in New Testament writings. Taken together, these two provide curious endpieces for the resurrection story, signifying the full extent of God's resurrection accomplishment. From the lowest hell to the highest heaven, there is no place where the power of the living Christ has not and does not reach. From bottom to top, the entire creation already knows his healing touch. Jesus is LORD of all!

We do ourselves a great favor by remembering that everything within the New Testament emerged from three or more decades of daily living and theological reflection by persons who lived with an unwavering conviction that the resurrected Jesus was still among them as a regal presence. These authors had felt the stealthy approach of old age and the sting of death and burying those they loved. And when they put pen to paper, they certainly were not ignorant of the continuing horrors within this world. Many of those horrors were aimed at and poured out on them and their friends because of this stubborn faith of theirs. Even so, on Sundays they gathered to worship and to sing hymns with defiant Easter joy to Jesus as the reigning LORD of all, and on weekdays they dared to profess "Jesus is LORD" in point-blank refutation of all the political and social intimidations of Caesar's lock-down world.

These Christ-followers were the first in the long procession of those who have understood Jesus to be the "hinge of history." In due time the calendars of the western world would be recalibrated in recognition of this historical shift. *Anno Domini*, the year of our LORD, became society's testimony to a new way of seeing history. In and through Jesus, the promised era of God's reign has dawned! The truth of that conviction still abides. Though "the battle is not [yet] done, Jesus who died shall be satisfied, and earth and heaven be one."[6]

NOTES

[1] An earlier form of this chapter appears as "Farewell to Saturday's World" in my book, *Finding the Gospel: A Pastor's Disappointment and Discovery* (Macon, GA: Nurturing Faith, 2020), 65-68.

[2] According to Matthew 27:52-53, resurrection phenomena began occurring moments after Jesus' death, but the other gospels report only the singular resurrection of Jesus three days later.

[3]"Death is the last weapon of the tyrant, and the point of the resurrection...is that death has been defeated. Resurrection is not the redescription of death; it is its overthrow and, with that, the overthrow of those whose power depends on it." N.T. Wright, *Surprised by Hope: Rethinking Heaven, the Resurrection, and the Mission of the Church* (New York: HarperOne, 2008), 50.

[4]From MLK's speech at Bishop Charles Mason Temple in Memphis, Tenn., on April 3, 1968.

[5]For those whose curiosity is great, I commend the discussions of N.T. Wright in *Surprised by Hope*, whose exegetical depth and historical detail exceed the boundaries of this meditation.

[6]Maltbie D. Babcock, "This Is My Father's World," 1901.

Abandon Hope, All Ye Who Enter Here

And I saw the dead, great and small, standing before the throne, and books were opened. Also another book was opened, the book of life. And the dead were judged according to their works, as recorded in the books. And the sea gave up the dead that were in it, Death and Hades gave up the dead that were in them, and all were judged according to what they had done. Then Death and Hades were thrown into the lake of fire. This is the second death, the lake of fire; and anyone whose name was not found written in the book of life was thrown into the lake of fire.

(Rev. 20:12-15)

I remember hearing this passage from the book of Revelation read aloud in church when I was a boy. However, I don't remember it—or its fellow-travelers—being what I'd call "Sunday morning" verses. Mostly, this kind of scary stuff was put into play by a professional evangelist on the closing Friday night of revival services. But whether it got a Sunday morning or a Friday night hearing, we all knew this was in the Book. And those evangelists, with sweat and storm, seared us with the fact that hell was as hot as heaven was cool, and we dare not leave the building without being sure our name was written in the Lamb's book of life.

I have not, for several decades, been a part of the church-world that traffics in that kind of speech or belief. But the feel of those sermons—always more frightening than the texts themselves—still plays in my head occasionally, mostly when I am talking with someone who still worships in places where hell is considered as real as the pulpit standing at the front of their church sanctuary. And every now and then, someone who I thought would have resolved their anxieties about hell surprises me with a comment revealing that the hopelessness of hell still haunts them. So, it seems fitting to offer some thoughts about the place whose gates the poet Dante imagined bore a sign declaring, "Abandon hope, all ye who enter here."

First, consider the kind of language that's being used in the New Testament's hell-talk. Apocalyptic is the technical word for that kind of language. We hear it especially in the Revelation to John, but in truth, *all* of the New Testament documents are set within an apocalyptic culture. That is, those times were filled with unrelieved tension. Raw and bitter polarities existed between Roman authorities and Jewish conviction, between rich and poor, between Jews and Gentiles, between "sinners" and the "righteous"—society tiptoed on knife edge. This climate produced its own style of literature, apocalyptic, a term that literally meant a revealing of the truth of things, an "unveiling" of reality.

To that end, apocalyptic literature drew striking verbal pictures of the players and motives, of their character and final destinies. It employed stark "either/or" and "with us/against us" options having exaggerated images (cosmic phenomena, menageries of grotesque beasts, bizarre statues, and lurid fates) to "reveal" the truth of the situation and its solemnity. You would not be far off the mark, therefore, to think of apocalyptic literature as dead-serious theological cartooning designed to expose and puncture the gaseous pretensions of the apparently powerful, to illustrate their certain downfall, and to reveal the rewards awaiting the stalwart.

The image of a "lake of fire" is well within this linguistic orbit, as is, for instance, the "great fixed chasm" in Jesus' parable of the rich man who died and found himself "in agony in Hades' flames" (Luke 16:19-31). In these texts, we are encountering apocalyptic language; we are hearing a way of talking, not receiving a snapshot of eternity. It is as erroneous to take this language literally as it is to ignore the damning significance of the rich man's indifference to the poor, or to glide over the frightful prospect of being "judged by what we have done" (as in the Revelation text). To insist on the "lake of fire" and the "great fixed chasm" as the message of these texts is to fixate on the cartoonist's artistry and ignore the cartoon's message. In both texts, the message is about ethics in the here and now, not housing arrangements in the hereafter.

Second, consider the question of who goes to hell. The evangelists of my youth were certain that all whose names were not written in the Lamb's book of life were going to hell. And they were also certain that the only way you could get your name recorded in that book was by accepting Jesus Christ as your personal savior. I have a faint recollection that one or two of these itinerant men of the cloth did seem aware of how many millions around the world were therefore headed straight to hell at any moment—but not because of anything they'd done, but because of something they'd never done: believe in a savior they'd never heard of! Which, even to my little boy way of figuring, was most unfair. Later it occurred to me that this also suggested that we humans weren't really saved by God's grace; we were saved by what we knew.

Then there was always Adolf Hitler. There was never, ever any doubt that he was going to hell—in our Christian hearts we hoped he was already there. And to this day, one of the best arguments for the existence of hell has his name on it. This argument insists there must be punishment; there must be a hell for persons whose evil is so clear and vicious. Without hell, the whole idea of right and wrong melts into nothing. You just can't let people such as Hitler off the hook and make it okay for them to be in the same heaven as a Mother Teresa!

And here, as I hinted, is where I still struggle. Adolf Hitler was one person. No doubt he was a diabolically inspired wretch of a person, but nonetheless he was just one man. The reason we remember him with such loathing is because multitudes of other people enabled him. They voted for him, they attended rallies endorsing his political agenda, they put on uniforms and even gave their lives to implement his megalomania and racist obsessions. And, disturbingly, almost all of these enablers were professing Christians! They were good Lutherans and Roman Catholics (the despised Jews made up less than one percent of Germany's population). I must assume therefore that all of them, to their own lights, "knew" Jesus as Savior. Does this mean that they receive a "get out of hell" card because of their professed faith in Jesus? That their complicity in a war that murdered six million Jews and killed fifty million more means nothing to God? And what are we to say of the pastors and priests, of the scholars and educators and journalists who not only failed to oppose Hitler's virulent racism, but also often championed it?

But push it even further. What are we to say of Martin Luther, the "rock star" of Germany's religious heritage? His writings are rife with some of the most anti-Semitic utterances in history. This man, so wonderfully insightful in so many ways, was abysmally blind to the racist venom he pushed upon his followers and the world at large. But the evil geniuses who became Hitler's inner circle certainly saw it and made good use of that anti-Semitism as a pious cover for their "final solution." Does Luther get a pass when we think of the crematoria of Auschwitz and Birkenau? Does his name in the book of life expunge all of this?

For that matter, what dare we say about some of the New Testament documents themselves—especially the gospel of John—that say such damning things about "the Jews" that Luther honestly believed his condemnation of "the Jews" was the teaching of scripture? You see, once we play the Hitler card as an example of why there must be a hell and say that a Christian profession of faith exempts us from it, we are setting up a scenario in which even the God who inspired holy scriptures can also be indicted for complicity in monstrous wickedness.

Consider a different but related dilemma. The clothing I am wearing was made in another country. World markets being what they are, it is more than likely that somewhere in the making and delivery of my garments some peasant, say in Cambodia, whose labor deserved dollars was paid pennies so that my clothing could be sold to me at a "good" price. And the uncomfortable truth, therefore, is that it could be justifiably said I am literally clothed in oppression of the poor! To be clear, I did not do this willfully or with personal malicious intent, but I am nonetheless a participant in an economic system that is not fair to all. I am an enabler of a system that mistreats some people for the profit of others, inextricably entangled in "the mystery of iniquity" that creates and sustains global inequity.

My point in all these illustrations is to draw attention to a metastasis of evil within this world that mocks our neat, hermetic categories of good/evil, pure/defiled, guilty/innocent. Admittedly, we need such categories to help us order our lives and make some sense of right and wrong. But ultimately the issues are more complex than our categories recognize, and I look to God one day to reveal a way of administering justice that transcends our present discernments. But for the time being, I remain very uncomfortable in saying that a simple "yes" to Jesus and a splash of holy water is all that is involved in one's name being written in the Lamb's book of life.

Finally, there is the issue of the character of God. Is God concerned with holy, all-merciful, all-knowing justice? Is God love? Is God good? Or, to put it most bluntly: Is God as good as Jesus? Personally, the bedrock of my entire faith is within my Yes answer to this last question. God is like Jesus! "He is the image of the invisible God…in him all the fullness of God was pleased to dwell" (Col. 1:15, 19). And if that be so, it certainly changes what we may rightly think of God.

There once was a very wealthy king who, gazing from a castle window, saw an exquisitely beautiful young lady in the marketplace below. She would be the perfect wife for his son. So off he goes into his kingdom, his son and soldiers in tow, to find the lovely lass. For he must sincerely invite her, not command her, to take his son's hand in marriage. When they finally find her, she is living in squalid circumstances, but the king nonetheless appeals to her to leave this pigsty and marry his son, where all the splendor of royalty will be at her command. There is, however, one condition. The king demands she make her decision before tomorrow noon! And if she delays, she will be cast into the darkest bowels of his dungeon and tortured forever and ever, without possibility of reconsideration. With that, the king and his retinue depart but not before the eager son says: "Please, do say yes. And be assured I will love you forever and always—but only until tomorrow noon."[1]

I cannot imagine Jesus ever letting anyone depart, let alone sending anyone, to the eternal damnation those preachers of my youth were so sure about. Yes, even Jesus said some very stern things—things that make me cringe—but if I listen and watch him through the entirety of his presence among us, I see a God-in-flesh worth loving and trusting with all I am and have. And the Holy One in whose name he came is one with him in all ways. That is my faith. And within that faith, and even within that scary "lake of fire" passage, I find hope. For only verses away from it I read that the gates of the New Jerusalem will never be shut (21:25).

Perhaps it will be the case that some people may forever reject the love of God, but it is clear that the door of God's mercy will never close. God's wrath, however we may define it and as merited as it may be, cannot be seen as the final expression of God's relationship with any of us. No, God is like Jesus. And in this Jesus, there was and is always hope! The gates of welcome will never be shut. So, I travel on in my belief that God really is as good as Jesus and I have hope that whatever hell means, it doesn't mean what I once was told.

NOTE

[1]Bradley Jersak, *A More Christlike God: A More Beautiful Gospel* (Pasadena, CA: Plain Truth Ministries, 2016).

We Shall Walk Through the Valley in Peace

The Lamb at the center of the throne will be their shepherd,
and he will guide them to springs of the water of life,
and God will wipe away every tear from their eyes.
(Rev. 7:17)

During the confinement days of our COVID-19 pandemic experience, I was asked to sit in on a virtual meeting of an adult Sunday School class of a church I once served as pastor. It was a delightful experience talking with old friends and discussing thoughts currently on our minds. But as we began wrapping up the session and exchanging final bits of personal news, one member spoke up, saying: "Before you go, may I ask a question? What do you think heaven is going to be like?"

Heaven had not been a part of any of the preceding discussion, so I was stunned by the question. My first reaction was to wonder if the questioner was facing a health crisis, and this was her way of informing the class without notifying the class. Then I wondered if, upon seeing my aging face on her laptop screen, she thought I looked half dead and supposed I surely must be giving heaven a second look. Finally, my surprise and wonderings dismissed, I realized her question, for whatever reason asked, was a valid one—always a valid one. What can I say about heaven? So, I stammered out something—I don't remember what—but my inability to remember what I said confirms that it certainly wasn't memorable.

In subsequent days I have come to realize I must say more. Unfortunately, some of us pastors say too little about death and what awaits us after it. (Others say too much, of course, but that's a topic for another day.) Our silence permits others to fill the void with ideas and images that often fail people in the hours of their deepest need. Denied the lively hope of biblical thought, the false hopes of fantasy and fear are free to reign. So, what can I say about heaven?

First, I can say that heaven is for real, but there is less about it in the Bible than many people may have thought.

Most certainly, the Old Testament has no clear teaching about a blessed, eternal life. Yes, Psalm 23 memorably concludes by saying: "I shall dwell in the house of the LORD for ever." But the expression "the house of the LORD" most likely refers to Jerusalem's temple, as it clearly does in a nearby verse: "One thing I asked of the LORD, that will I seek after: to live in the house of the LORD all the days of my life, to behold the beauty of the LORD, and to inquire in his temple" (27:4). And "for ever" is the way the 1611 King James Version translated a Hebrew expression that we now know can better be translated as "my whole life long" or "for length of days." "For many long years" is the way the Jewish Publication Society renders it in their translation for today's readers.[1] Psalm 23 is indeed a comforting, assuring ode to the unfailing companionship of God throughout life, but no, there is no promise of heaven, in our usual connotation, within it.

Another Old Testament "heaven" passage I have long loved is Psalm 73:22-26. Its anchor verse, in the King James Version, says: "Thou shalt guide me with thy counsel, and afterword receive me to glory." The New International Version doubles down on that latter phrase, translating it as "you will take me into glory." But the New Revised Standard Version more starkly says "you will receive me with honor" and the Jewish translation, granting that it could be translated as "and afterward receive me with glory," prefers to restate it in the past tense and render it as "You...led me toward honor," adding a footnote that the meaning of the Hebrew is "uncertain."[2]

The verse following adds this: "Whom have I in heaven but you? And there is nothing on earth that I desire other than you" (25). Though a Christian reading of this passage may see "our" heaven in it, in the context of this psalm the "heaven/earth" reference means that the LORD above is the psalmist's all-sufficient hope and strength today. Once again, a verse that might be taken as an assurance of a life in heaven becomes less certain upon closer inspection. We may, with Christian imagination, read our concepts into this and other psalms, but they were not written with this understanding. The idea of heaven that Christian sensibilities seek is *almost* there, but not really. It remains in the shadows.

We might expect that all of this changes once we come to the New Testament. Indeed, it does—but not wholly. Coming some four hundred years after the latest Old Testament writing, the New Testament does confidently speak of a life after death and of a waiting heaven. But if the question is asked of the Gospels, as it was of me, "What do you think heaven is like?" the silence that follows is significant.

The one glorious exception to this silence is found in John 14:1-3 where Jesus seeks to comfort the troubled hearts of his disciples when they had to confront the fact of his departure.[3] Here there can be little question that Jesus is talking about what happens after death and what heaven is like. "In my Father's house," he says, "there are many dwelling places. If it were not so, would I have told you that I go to prepare a place for you? And if I go and prepare a place for you, I will come again and will take you to myself, so that where I am, there you may be also."

This statement permits me to say a second, New Testament truth about heaven: It is for real, and Jesus speaks of it clearly.

Jesus begins by saying his death means he is going to a "place" he calls "my Father's house." So, heaven is a "place," a destination, the residence of the Creator of the ends of the earth. But Jesus doesn't speak of its manicured lawns or balconies or spacious rooms. For how can you speak of the "house" of the One whom even the heaven of heavens cannot contain? Others may speak of golden streets and pearly gates, but not Jesus. For him, it is enough that this "place," this heaven, is "my Father's house." Though it appears on no map, it is no less a "place" for that; it is, in fact, the most real "place" of all.

In a different New Testament passage (Rev. 21:2), this "place" is called "the holy city," perhaps because, unlike the open roads in those days, cities were safer. This "place" will be a safe place, its walls protecting its residents. This city also has a name: "new Jerusalem." The ancient city, believed to be God's earthly residence and the site of God's instruction and worship, is now "new" and is "the home of God…among mortals" (v. 3). The holy city visited in pilgrimage is now the "place" to be enjoyed forever as a fellow resident with God.

Lest the urban imagery disappoint some, this city also has a river flowing through it with a fruit-bearing tree on either side of it (22:1-5). This city is no concrete jungle; it is a garden "place," too. My breath has often been taken away by the beauty of many garden places on earth. Is it inexcusable childishness to imagine this terrestrial beauty is but a preface to the greater beauty of this garden "place"? Too, the leaves of the never-out-of-season fruit tree within this garden are "for the healing of the nations." Ancient enmity between nations and peoples is no more. The warring spirit finds healing in the beauty of this "place."

So, "my Father's house" is a safe "place," a new "place," a God "place," a beautiful/healing "place," a "place" where our restlessness may find a home and the heart find its healing. C.S. Lewis once conjectured that the most frequently heard word in heaven will be "Ohhh!" spoken either in astonished understanding of the why of suffering in this life, or perhaps in response to the unutterable beauty of the place Jesus called "my Father's house."

Next we read that Jesus is going to prepare "a place for you" within the "many dwelling places" in his Father's house. Contrary to there being "no place" for him when he came to us at Bethlehem (Luke 2:7), God has many dwelling places awaiting us. "Plenty good room" is the promise.

Jesus himself is said to be the chief preparation officer, the architect and designer who has gone ahead to "prepare a place" in this commodious place. Earlier he had spoken of even the hairs of our head being known, and of his being the shepherd who knows his sheep by name. This being so, it is unlikely that a place prepared by him "for you" will be generic, cookie-cutter cubicles for Resident X or Y or Z.

Finally, he crowns his revelation with the promise that he will "come again" and "take you to myself that where I am, there you may be also." Jesus doesn't describe the kind or manner or means of his "coming," but promises that in whatever way this mortal life ends, Jesus will be the one who "takes" his own to the Father's house. Not some deputy, but "I will come again and take you to myself."

In this life we are promised that nothing can separate us from the *love* of God; in the life to come we are promised that nothing can separate us from the *presence* of God, for "where I am, there you will be also." Those who find Christ's presence worth seeking on earth will find this new place heaven; all others may find it hell. As for those whose main heavenly goal is to be reunited and meet lost loved ones, this word hints that the better thought is to think of it as the place to meet and be with God!

This is all I know to say of heaven, all my feeble imagination can presently draw from the promises I find in scripture. This then is the scope of my hope, and, like all hope, is rooted in these promises and comes alive in imagination. But whatever I might say is going to under-represent the reality, for "what no eye has seen, nor ear heard, nor the human heart conceived, what God has promised for those who love him" (1 Cor. 2:9).

There is, however, a final thing I must say about heaven. And here I must confess that my truest anxiety about all this is not about the "place," but about the entrance to it, the getting there—the act of dying. Of course, I know Jesus pledges to "come and take you to myself." But quite honestly, "when I have fears that I may cease to be,"[4] my spirit hears Jesus' pledge most powerfully through a simple spiritual. That song repetitiously affirms:

> We shall walk through the valley in peace, in peace.
> We shall walk through the valley in peace.
> For if Jesus himself shall be our leader,
> We shall walk through the valley in peace.

I find comfort, deep comfort, in the hope that when I someday must walk through the valley of death's shadow, and there feel the mists of Jordan upon my face, "I won't have to cross Jordan alone." For Jesus himself shall be my leader in that valley, through those waters, and all the way to the "place" he has prepared.

Countless times across a half-century I have read beautiful words at gravesides for others' benefit, hoping that one or two of those words might find a lodging place in the sad hearts around me. Recently, recalling one of those words, my own heart was stunned by the strength and beauty of its message: "The Lamb who is at the center of the throne will shepherd them and lead them to springs of life-giving water, and God will wipe away every tear from their eyes."

These words, spoken by one of the elders in heaven about those who have come out of "the great ordeal," are applicable to all whose ordeal is still ongoing. They declare that at the center of what lasts forever—the throne of God—that at the very center of the throne of Forever, is the Lamb who was slain and raised up by God.

If, in our ordeal, we ever wonder what really lasts, we are to remember that it is not power or fame or wealth or pleasure, but the simplicity and goodness of Jesus that endures forever. All that he was, now reigns at the center of the Eternal.

If, in our ordeal, we ever question what it will be like to live in the Father's house, we are to remember whose beauty, vitality, and gentleness reigns at its center.

If, in our ordeal, we ever wonder how we shall get to that "place," we are to remember that the Lamb will be our shepherd. Because Jesus himself shall be our leader, there is no need for fear.

If, in our ordeal, we ever wonder what shall become of us in that "place," we are to remember that at its gates are "springs of life-giving water" where life-beaten, death-dried souls may drink their fill. And then...

...then look up and behold the One waiting there, towel in hand, ready to wipe away every tear from our eyes! But can this possibly be? That God—the God of far-flung galaxies and the God of Golgotha's bloody brow—might be waiting there, kneeling to wipe away every tear from a sinner's eyes? What tears might we have in that moment?

...tears of joyful disbelief at the wonder, of this moment, of this God?

...tears of embarrassment for how slow we were to trust and follow the Lamb?

...tears of regret for the harm we did and the good we could have done?

...tears of gratitude for all who helped us on this journey?

Questions still churn within me about what death and heaven will be like. But if "my Father's house" holds this at its entrance, can I not tell my anxious heart to hush and to trust God for all that is within?

"Night is drawing nigh. For all that has been—Thanks! To all that shall be—Yes!"[5]

NOTES

[1] *TANAKH: A New Translation of the Holy Scriptures According to the Traditional Hebrew Text* (Philadelphia: The Jewish Publication Society, 1985), 1132.

[2] Ibid., 1193.

[3] I am painfully aware of the difficulty of "quoting" Jesus as though a stenographer had been present to capture his every word. But my inability to affirm that "Jesus said" precisely this or that does not keep me from saying that the resurrected Jesus speaks today through those printed words. He speaks through, if not in, his "words."

[4] John Keats, "When I Have Fears That I May Cease to Be," 1848.

[5] Dag Hammarskjold, *Markings* (New York: Alfred A. Knopf, 1998), 89.

A Provisional Conclusion

May the God of hope fill you with all joy and peace in believing,
so that you may abound in hope by the power of the Holy Spirit.
(Rom. 15:13)

So, after all these words and pages, what is the end of the matter? What is hope? In two paragraphs and four sentences, here is the best I can offer as an answer to that question—for now:

> In broadest scope, hope is the fragile birthright of every human, freshly re-given each day as God's motivation gift calling us to become our truest self and to discover our greatest joy. Hope is also a gift held in communal trust by the human family, and it flourishes only as we extend it to one another in faith and love.
>
> In Christian construal, hope is our confidence in the steadfast love of God to hold and sustain us through life and to receive us in death just as God did for our LORD, Jesus. And because we believe God raised him from the dead, our hope is that through his resurrection we and all creation are now being, and one day will fully be, raised to new life.

Definitions such as this sometimes help me grasp a subject more firmly, but just as often they leave me wishing the writer had clarified this or that detail. So, the following paragraphs offer a few interpretive comments about these definitions and then go on to suggest how hope may be related to its frequently named companions, faith and love.[1]

The first of these definitions is my attempt to speak of hope in a universal sense, and as such it has an eye upon the societal and political dimensions of hope. While not muting the sacred character of hope, it speaks more of our shared public task of fostering hope within others, rather than ever being a party to its diminishment. For some Christians this may be heard as a call to evangelize—and that response certainly has its place. But in many situations I believe such witnessing needs to begin with solidarity with those who struggle daily to keep hope alive. Hope is not solely a spiritual, inward virtue; it is also a call to civic service and social engagement. To speak of hope without actively seeking to aid those who are without hope is to propagate a fraud. To the degree we are negligent in advancing our neighbors' hope, we diminish our own.

At the same time, for the Christian, hope is a sustaining and motivating spiritual dynamic that finds its living center in the person and gospel of Jesus Christ. If hope could be said to have a face, that face for Christians would be the face of Jesus. In him we discover the coalescence of ancient stories and spiritual insight that brings us daily hope, societal hope, and also hope for eternity. Through faith in him and because of love for him, Jesus' followers continue to experience a "hope that does not disappoint us, because God's love has been poured into our hearts" (Rom. 5:5).

Surely a portion of why hope is such a profound reality for Christians is found within St. Paul's famous linkage of hope with faith and love: "And now faith, hope, and love abide, these three; and the greatest of these is love" (1 Cor. 13:13). In these words Paul combines three powerful dynamics, any one of which can transform life, but when united they create an incalculable cumulative force for noble living. Note, however, that Paul places hope between the towering giants of faith and love—and a quick glance at any library's holdings will reveal that mountains of books have been written about the giants of faith and love—but not so many about their little companion, hope. I would argue, though, that hope stands just as tall as its neighbors.

Consider this assertion by giving thought to how we use these words. No doubt it is only a quirk of the English language but of these three, only faith is not used as a verb. Of course, we may informally say we are "faithing" something, but the dictionaries and grammar books will remind us that this way of speaking is not according to the rules. If we wish to speak of faith in an active sense, we must use words such as trusting or believing. Faith, as a word, retains its character as a noun, as a thing. But this is not so with hope and love. They are used as both verbs and nouns. Both have an active dimension to them that the word faith does not.

Building upon this simple lexical observation, think then of faith as being the root system for the flowers of hope and love growing from faith's stem. A root system is usually a below-surface phenomenon, an essential, though out-of-sight, supportive matrix. In like manner, faith, in and of itself, is invisible. Its presence is seen only as hope and love reveal faith's presence and do faith's work. Because of faith's rich nutrients, hope and love have nourishing soil and supportive roots for their flowering. Each has its own distinct role, yet these three "abide" together as one interdependent unit.

One may also think of hope and love as the two faces of faith. Hope is faith's face when we are dealing with time and history, with the dailyness of life and its demands. When faith confronts obstacles, deals with frustration, and requires patience, and persistence—especially in times of loss and change and incompleteness—then faith looks like hope. Hope relates to how we navigate the passage of time. We might even hazard a rephrasing: We walk by *hope* and not by sight—realizing, of course, that hope refers to faith's time-oriented posture.

Correspondingly, one may think of love as faith's face when dealing with people. It is the face we are talking about when we interact with others with whom we share life's passage. Love expresses faith's conviction that all these others are made in God's image and worthy of our respect and compassion. If hope relates to how we handle our circumstances, then love relates to how we handle our relationships. Hope deals with our inward orientation to life's journey, while love deals with our outward orientation toward our fellow travelers.

If we view these three in the manner I am suggesting, we may see that in the Christian linkage of faith and hope and love we are given a distinct, God-centered way (faith) of interpreting the days of our life (hope) and of relating to the people of our life (love). Each facet nurtures and challenges the others, and in so doing a holistic synergy of grace envelops us.

But in this linkage there also lurks a stern rebuttal of the popular refrain: "I don't care what you believe; all that matters is how you behave." This familiar sentiment summarily dismisses faith as superfluous and exalts deeds as most essential. And it takes no savant to understand why. We are up to our necks in the hypocrisy of those whose faith never yields the anticipated behavioral fruits.

Perhaps the Apostle Paul might even be wrongly heralded as the champion of this school of thought. After all, when writing to the dysfunctional church in Corinth, he said that "the greatest of these is love." But more careful consideration leads us to know that there is more to Paul's thought than just that one memorable line. All of his letters to young churches are notable for their combination of ethics and doctrine, the interplay of faith and behavior. Getting the faith straight was of great concern for Paul. And, although he did say that love trumps all, Paul had no intention of elevating love to the detriment of good faith as a basis for that love. Corinth's need was not the minimizing of faith, but the development of good, nurturing faith. For faith has everything to do with whom and how we love and what we hope and work for.

Our failures in love and hope do not expose the irrelevance of faith; rather, they only underscore how desperately we need healthy, humble, truthful faith. Hope and love cannot long endure without the guidance and nutrients of this kind of faith. These three are meant to grow and dance together! If we wish to avoid becoming a "cut flower" culture, having severed ourselves from our root system, all three must be tended.

Finally, I relinquish my pen to the Apostle of Jesus, this man named Paul, who was "afflicted in every way, but not crushed; perplexed, but not driven to despair; persecuted, but not forsaken; struck down, but not destroyed" (2 Cor. 4:8-9)—to this man who knew so much more about hope than I ever will. But I want you to hear him through the language of another great hoper, J. B. Phillips. Phillips (1906–1982) was an Anglican minister who wrote several remarkably good books, and even translated much of the Bible into the everyday language of his times. But he did much of this while relentlessly contending with the grey fog of depression, a soul emptiness that could be managed only by faith, hope, and love. Hear then, as a last word, how this gentle hoper gave contemporary expression to two of Paul's most beautiful paragraphs about hope.

In my opinion, whatever we may have to go through now is less than nothing compared to the magnificent future God has planned for us. The whole creation is on tiptoe to see the wonderful sight of the [children] of God coming into their own. The world of creation cannot as yet see reality, not because it chooses to be blind, but because in God's purpose it has been so limited—yet it has been given hope. And the hope is that in the end the whole of created life will be rescued from the tyranny of change and decay, and have its share in that magnificent liberty which can only belong to the children of God!

It is plain to anyone with eyes to see that at the present time all created life groans in a sort of universal travail. And it is plain, too, that we who have a foretaste of the Spirit are in a state of painful tension, while we wait for that redemption of our bodies which will mean that at last we have realized our full [stature] in him. We were saved by this hope, but in our moments of impatience let us remember that hope always means waiting for something that we do not yet possess. But if we hope for something we cannot see, then we must settle down to wait for it in patience. (Rom. 8:18-25)[2]

NOTES

[1] See note 1 of "The Grandest Gamble," pp 55-56.

[2] *The New Testament in Modern English* (New York: The Macmillan Company, 1964). J.B. Phillips reports in part his struggle with depression in *The Price of Success: An Autobiography* (Wheaton, IL: Harold Shaw Publishers, 1984) and recounted in more detail by Vera Phillips and Edwin Robertson, *J.B. Phillips: The Wounded Healer* (Grand Rapids: Wm. B. Eerdmans Publishing Co. Publishing, 1985).

CPSIA information can be obtained
at www.ICGtesting.com
Printed in the USA
BVHW060823271221
624876BV00013B/669